DEVOUT
SCEPTICS

DEVOUT SCEPTICS

CONVERSATIONS ON

FAITH AND DOUBT

WITH

BEL MOONEY

Hodder & Stoughton
LONDON SYDNEY AUCKLAND

British Library Cataloguing in Publication Data
A record for this book is available from the British Library

ISBN 0 340 86202 5

Typeset in Garamond by Avon DataSet Ltd,
Bidford-on-Avon, Warwickshire

Printed and bound in Great Britain by
Clays Ltd., St Ives plc, Bungay, Suffolk

The paper and board used in this paperback are natural recyclable
products made from wood grown in sustainable forests.
The manufacturing processes conform to the environmental
regulations of the country of origin.

Hodder & Stoughton
A Division of Hodder Headline Ltd
338 Euston Road
London NW1 3BH
www.madaboutbooks.com

For

Malcolm Love

Strange is our situation here upon earth.
Each of us comes for a short visit, not knowing why,
yet sometimes seeking to divine a purpose.

Albert Einstein, *Living Philosophies*

Two things fill the mind with ever new and increasing
awe and admiration the more frequently and
continuously reflection is occupied with them:
the starred heaven above me
and the moral law within me.

Immanuel Kant, *Critique of Practical Reason*

Contents

A Note on the Text

People often ask for transcripts of radio programmes which have moved them or made them think. Quite apart from the expense of such a service (which is why it is now rarely available) it can be less than satisfactory, simply because the spoken word has a different rhythm to the word on the page, and to read a literal transcript may not revive the original programme in the way the listener hoped. But sometimes it can. To offer what is in effect an 'anthology' of the five series (to date) of *Devout Sceptics* on Radio 4 goes some way to answering that need expressed by so many listeners, who want to be able to contemplate at leisure some of the thoughts and anecdotes of our distinguished guests. Out of a total of thirty-two programmes I had the difficult task of selecting twenty for inclusion in the main body of this book, using variety as the chief criterion. The other twelve are represented by quotation in my introduction. So all who have taken part are here, in one way or another.

Restrictions of space then forced me to edit conversations already edited for transmission. Sometimes people underestimate the amount of work behind an apparently simple broadcast discussion. For one thing, putative interviewees usually have to be reassured that they really do have something to offer on this deeply personal subject of faith and doubt. After all, writers may talk about writing and politicians about matters of state, but who talks much about

God? From the moment a guest arrives at the studio, the producer Malcolm Love and I work to create an atmosphere where such a conversation will be both relaxed and searching. We may record up to fifty minutes (very occasionally more), and Malcolm will then shape that into the finished programme. Often many of my questions/prompts will be lost, but that doesn't matter. Sometimes whole chunks of talk have to be cut, because of the tyranny of the clock. But what results is, I believe, quietly terrific radio.

Here I have included the essence of each programme, editing some much more than others, for reasons of space. One or two are almost complete as broadcast, because we had such a response. Because speech is peppered with conversational phrases like 'I mean' and 'sort of' and 'I think', which do not read well, I have edited them out, while retaining the flavour of the individual's speech and the integrity of the broadcast. Similarly, repetitions of 'and' oil our conversations but look awkward on paper, and so I have pruned them to make the text a more graceful read. I have also omitted still more of my comments and questions: in truth, my interest as a broadcaster is discovery, not display, and so I welcome near-invisibility.

I talked about *Devout Sceptics* to the Reverend Ernie Rea, then Head of BBC Religion, and I am grateful to him for taking the idea to Michael Green, then Controller of Radio 4, who commissioned the first three series. The current Controller, Helen Boaden, recommissioned the series at the coveted 9 a.m. slot, which brought it to an even larger audience, and we appreciate her enthusiasm for the subject. The dedication to this book speaks for itself: Malcolm Love was born into the Baptist faith, embraced it with enthusiasm, became a pastor in Battersea and taught evangelicalism to others for more than ten years. In trying to square dogma with real people's lives he made a slow journey from certainty to doubt and joined the ranks of the devout sceptics. We make a good team. As always, Jonathan Dimbleby is a constant support and source of wisdom, while Georgie Grindlay and Jackson Kingman prepared the transcriptions with involvement as well as efficiency. Amy Tan was generous with her permission. Most of all, I am deeply grateful to all those guests who shared their questions and thoughts about God and the human spirit – through me – with the ever-receptive, intelligent and loyal Radio 4 audience. May the conversations never cease, as we try to make sense of who we are and why we are here, even in the darkest times.

Introduction

Some days, although we cannot pray, a prayer utters itself...

Carol Ann Duffy

The idea for *Devout Sceptics* came to me some years ago when reading Sir Leslie Stephens's *An Agnostic's Apology* (1931). The phrase is his – an oxymoron as potent as 'bitter-sweet'. Irritated by organised religion, he nevertheless acknowledged the sense of the numinous within the human spirit and the longing for faith which may result: 'We wish for spiritual food and are to be put off with these ancient mummeries of forgotten dogma.' I immediately identified with his description of humankind as 'dimly discerning light enough for our daily needs, but hopelessly differing whenever we attempt to describe the ultimate origin or end of our paths'. Throughout history men and women have been aware of the Other: a dimension of spirit which transcends the mundane. But they may not name it God. It seemed a promising subject for discussion on the best medium for such things: radio.

Since I am endlessly fascinated by the roads people take towards faith or doubt, it seems appropriate to describe my own. I was not brought up in a religious household, but my grandmother Ann Mooney had a simple but profound belief in God and would often take me to a Congregational church on Edge Lane, Liverpool, where we vied with one another trying to hit high notes in the hymns. By the age of eleven I had developed a taste for candles and gilt, as well as for walking in churchyards, brooding about death, wondering where we all *go*. As an emotional fourteen-year-old I was drawn into the warm family of the Wesley Road Methodist Church in Trowbridge, Wiltshire, and sincerely believed that God and I had found each other for ever. The social inclusiveness at the heart of nonconformism was one of the factors that propelled me towards politics, and by seventeen *angst* over the Bomb replaced any longing for the bread of heaven.

I rejected the idea of God, believing that no God of Love could preside over a world so apparently lacking in that commodity. Like countless others before and since, I demanded to know how the Almighty could have witnessed the Holocaust, or Hiroshima. No explanations could suffice. Since then, however, the seeking for him /her/it has been like a guilty secret inside me, with no curtained confessional in which to whisper. When a bereavement left me bleak and bitter, I would skulk into churches to light candles for my baby – a devout ritual usually accompanied by silent rage and insults hurled against the God I steadfastly denied. I *needed* to believe – to rail about being forsaken under a heaven which thunderously accepted the blame. In longing for God I wanted a scapegoat: a convenient deity who could at once be castigated for causing suffering and thanked for providing the hope which might alleviate it.

Now it seems more interesting to consider the nature of that longing: a slow and patient exploration in which the loneliness and doubts of the journey are far more important than any ecstatic arrival at Ithaca. While I may still envy those whose faith is strong, there are (sadly) many proofs that external religious observance need have no effect on moral behaviour, while the atheist can be morally upright with no faith other than a sense of duty towards humankind. In a sense this book adds up to a celebration of doubt as a positive force.

One of my favourite literary anecdotes was told by F.W.H. Myers about George Eliot. He described how, in 1873, they walked in the Fellows' garden at Trinity and she, 'taking as her text the three words which have been used so often as the inspiring trumpet-calls of men – the words *God, Immortality, Duty* – pronounced with terrible earnestness, how inconceivable was the *first*, how unbeliev-able the *second*, and yet how peremptory and absolute the *third'*. George Eliot renounced the faith of her father, but her 'religion of humanity', her commitment to 'other people's wants and sorrows', was as strong and sacred as any theological dogma. She had no sympathy for arid free-thinking but believed that the longing for God, that impulse upwards and outwards, was as profound an expression of the human spirit as her own belief that 'pity and fairness embrace the utmost delicacies of the moral life'.

Most (if not all) of those who agreed to be guests on five series of *Devout Sceptics* would have applauded George Eliot's combination of reason with reverence, when reverence means (to over-simplify) trying to do good. The novelist, film-maker and political activist Tariq Ali summed it up thus: 'I know you're born, you live, you love, you work, you produce children or not, children produce children, and then you die. And that's that. So it's what you *do* in this life that really matters.' Anita Roddick, founder of The Body Shop and human rights campaigner, expressed a similar thought more lyrically: 'I don't want to go on thinking about the Almighty or God. For me it is personified in this inescapable joy, and the nature of friendships and the family, and giving birth – the sensuousness . . . And the *humanity*. Working in Bosnia and seeing how the humanity can equal the dark side – how the natural sense of love is displayed stranger to stranger.'

At first my definition of a 'devout sceptic' was somebody who has glimmerings of faith even if he or she rejects the established Church. Yet we were forced to broaden the scope. The opera and theatre director and polymath Dr Jonathan Miller defined himself as a passionate sceptic – devout about his very atheism. Yet he did not reject my use of the term 'experience of the sacred' and replied: 'I think most people, unless they're really very oafish clods, find there is something deeply mysterious and mind-stopping – and in some ways thought-stopping – about the business of being alive at all. It's a very paradoxical state of affairs that something made of such unpromising material can be self-conscious and see itself as being in a world that is larger than itself, and having a large, dark periphery which cannot be penetrated.' Similarly, the psychotherapist Dorothy Rowe, another atheist, said, 'Whatever metaphysical beliefs we hold they're a central part of our way of thinking and a central part of determining what we do. Everybody has metaphysical beliefs because there are some things in your life that you can explain in a logical and rational way and there are other things where it's impossible to do that – because you can't get the evidence. Nobody knows what death is. Nobody knows what the purpose of life may be but they are things that we think about – and so we work out a set of beliefs.'

Devout sceptics are seekers who won't trust the maps they have been given but know there is a destination towards which to stumble, even if it proves to be the place they began at and (to invoke T.S. Eliot) they know it for the first time. What *is* religious feeling, or (to be less specific) a sense of the numinous? To those raised in the Judeo-Christian tradition it will presuppose a revelation from one God, maintained by the sacred community of the Church. But many faiths have worshipped more than one god, while some have worshipped no god at all. A growing interest in Buddhism, for example, is notable among my contemporaries as well as the younger generation. The actress-turned-psychotherapist Pamela Stephenson explained: 'I turned my back on Christianity when I was in my mid-twenties and actually found Buddhism a wonderful philosophy to become involved with. There was the fact that I could at last feel I had begun life as a wonderful piece of creation, that a person doesn't have to struggle every day to overcome darkness and sin. That was such a relief to learn – and to feel a lot of inner strength, inner peace through practical things like meditation.'

The actor John Cleese quoted extensively from the Tibetan master Sogyal Rinpoche, and explained: 'There are two different approaches and, with the exception of a few mystics who are slightly embarrassing and swept into the corner, the Western approach has nearly always been that we must try and understand everything with our minds, and basically argue about how many angels we can get on the head of a pin. That can become pretty sterile.' Rejecting dogma-based religion he too was drawn to meditation, went to see the Dalai Lama, and received advice from a Lama on how to meditate. After discussing these techniques Cleese added, 'It's so hard for us in the West not to edit our thoughts. Somebody once said to me it's like watching a windscreen wiper on your car: you know that they're going but you don't actually have to watch them – you look beyond them. The Lama told me, "Out of this quietness slowly arises your real being. You'll experience an aspect of yourself which is more genuine and more authentic, the real you. As you go deeper you begin to discover and connect with your fundamental goodness." Of course, the big difference between the East and the West is that in the West we're told that we're fundamentally rather sinful and in the East they believe that you're fundamentally good.'

In the arts, popular culture and interior design, the crossing of conventional boundaries between East and West has enriched people's lives in ways that defy analysis. One might mock that ubiquitous decorating trope, the head of Buddha, but who is to know what power emanates from such images? Who is to say that the ritual burning of joss sticks, lighting of candles and scattering of crystals in the home, far from being New Age nonsense, may not have an effect of calming and uplifting the soul equal to that of the 'smells and bells' in the Catholic Church? Cynics despise this 'pick 'n' mix' attitude to religion as the need for an insurance policy – a mixture of New-Agey fluffiness with the hope for a visitation from a divine Man from the Pru. But who cares? The Vatican may warn against it ('The challenge of New Age religiosity cannot be underestimated . . . when understanding of the content of Christian faith is weak, some seek answers elsewhere') but I felt greatly liberated the day I realised there's nothing wrong with being comfortable in the hippy-chic coat of many colours.

The point is, we cannot *know*. The spirit of the modern has been to question everything, but that is not necessarily at odds with a sense of the religious, as many of the conversations in *Devout Sceptics* made clear. I have already pointed out how agnosticism may be fuelled by the profoundest moral sense; similarly, four elements of secular life today (our conversations showed again and again) can lead to glimmerings of the divine: scientific knowledge, awareness of the environment, the wide availability of the arts, and the psychological study of human nature.

The picture of the universe brought to us by modern scientific knowledge is one which renders the traditional religious attribute of awe entirely appropriate. Pascal's mediaeval vision of the sky – its silence and immensity truly terrifying – might well be shared by the modern astronomer, whose instruments, more powerful than ever, lead him to the outer reaches of Kant's 'starred heaven' to find . . . infinity. And humility, perhaps. The great Artificial Intelligence guru, Igor Aleksander, Professor of Neural Systems Engineering at Imperial College London, told me: 'God is a fixed-point concept which is surrounded by religion, and God in one religion is slightly different from God in others. But I see a fairly relaxed relationship between religion and science which over the centuries has had a dynamic which makes sense. Science is there to tell us what's been discovered through a logical process of inquiry; religion is there to allow us to cope with things that don't necessarily have a logical explanation. And a lot of things in life are totally mysterious, including our own consciousness. Why is it that we're born, we die? What causes emotions – and so on? Religion gives us strategies to cope with all that.'

One of the most brilliant mathematicians and physicists in the world, Professor Sir Roger Penrose, concluded our discussion with this magnificently hesitant statement: 'I think the more we learn about the universe, the more point we see to it. I'm not sure how to fill that statement out, I just think that when one uses the word "mystery" it implies there is somehow more going on than just the result of random occurrences. I think there is – something. Whether one calls it a purpose in the ordinary sense of that word, I don't know – but there's something more there. Yes.' Thus physics can lead one along the path to metaphysics.

From the starry sky to a grain of sand, nature is a constant source of wonder, and the breath of wonder transforms the soul. Michael Eavis, Somerset farmer and founder of the world-famous Glastonbury Festival, spoke for many people when he said simply: 'People get inspiration from the natural world, don't they? The more you walk up the Tor, and watch the sun setting over Sedgemoor Valley, you see so much beauty and find so much inspiration. Whether or not that's divine . . . I don't think it is, really . . .' The writer and agony aunt Irma Kurtz described an epiphany on a beach by a bird reserve in Mexico: 'There was nobody but me, and a surf too strong to swim in. One day I sat very still and looked at the water, and a pelican came so close I could feel the air displaced in front of my face. It sounds very Buddhist, but I thought, "I'm not here any more. I'm *in it*. The edge of me has melted. This is wonderful. I'm *in it*." ' She concluded, 'I would call that a spiritual experience,' and went on, 'We're living a miracle. The chances of our being here are so slim, that's a miracle. And so from the moment you are born you are living a miracle.'

Again and again, people who profess a rational agnosticism will express humble awe at the beauty of the natural world, whether in a simple field of daffodils or a high peak in the Andes. The pantheist or pagan might smile in the knowledge of what this implies; certainly, according to Aboriginal or Native American culture, the spirit is 'far more deeply interfused' (in Wordsworth's phrase), leaving no doubt as to the source of that awe – and love. It is arguable that, more than ever today, a large number of people regard the protection of that holy natural world against the forces of human greed and ignorance as being as important – and religious – a crusade as any. Though church attendance is falling, human beings are experiencing epiphanies among the trees and hills, or showing, by their respect for the animal kingdom and the most minute eco-systems, an awareness that God's created beings are of equal worth.

A sense of the sacred may be found in a field; it may be inspired by contemplation of the great rose window at Chartres. Centuries of culture have provided images of God, but the awe goes back much further. Men and women 'invented' religion at the same time as they invented art, both perhaps an expression of primitive wonder at earthquake, wind and fire, and (the other side of the coin) the beneficence of food. The Greeks knew 'it' as 'unsearchable wisdom' or relentless Fate; Thomas Hardy visualised a careless providence or destiny which makes of the human show a laughing stock.

Yet works of art created for the greater glory of God may serve to remind the humanist of what the human soul is capable. I have no doubt that agnostics like myself tiptoe towards the deity while listening to music. It is easy to decry the worst excesses of popular culture; the fact remains that Art (and I capitalise it, as I sometimes capitalise God) has the power to make the universe shiver. One could argue that more and more people are going to art galleries and museums, listening to poetry on Radio 4, and joining serious reading groups, while the wide availability of budget CDs and the proliferation of arts festivals mean that the arts impinge on our lives as never before. The jazz singer, art collector and avowed atheist George Melly made this 'confession': 'Let me say something – I feel awe, and very like religious awe, in front of certain paintings, by Piero della Francesca particularly. These are paintings of great radiance and simplicity, done by a believer – and I cannot but be awed in front of them, especially the one in which Christ is baptised. It does slightly throw me that I am so impressed by pictures painted with a specific religious reason, and to express a faith.' He went on to discuss the sense of mystery in Surrealism, and added, 'I find it in Dickens, who is able to make people, landscapes, weather into a mystery – something beyond itself, beyond its meaning.'

The actress Sheila Hancock was another guest who spoke eloquently of the effect of art during her search for a faith: 'I could be moved and comforted and delighted by listening to Bach or Elgar or Rachmaninov – just as moved as I would be by a religious service. Because – it is living proof. When I listen to the *St Matthew Passion* I am profoundly stirred, moved and elevated, which is what a lot of people look for in religion.' Speaking personally, I am one of those who can stand in front of the Wilton Diptych and hear the sound of angels' wings, worship the glory of the everyday in a Vermeer, or see in Picasso's *Guernica* as powerful a denunciation of evil and expression of compassion for suffering humanity as I have found in any scriptures.

The psychological study of human nature, a twentieth-century discipline as well as a commonplace in the 'mind and body' sections of modern newspapers, perpetually reaffirms the value of the individual and reiterates the values of compassion and forgiveness preached by Jesus of Nazareth and emanating from the smile on the face of the Buddha. George Eliot believed that 'our moral progress may be measured by the degree in which we sympathise with individual suffering and individual joy'. I do not believe that any of the people who have agreed to be guests on *Devout Sceptics* would disagree with this. On the contrary, they would be glad of the approbation of one of our wisest commentators on religious affairs, Karen Armstrong, who writes: 'Humanism is itself a religion without God . . . Our ethical, secular ideal has its own disciplines of mind and heart and gives people the means of finding faith in the ultimate meaning of human life that were once provided by the more conventional religions.'

Why the search? Why make such an effort, when we most of us cannot answer Gauguin's final questions: 'Who are we? Where have we come from? Where are we going?' But for all those who agree to be classed as a devout sceptic the perpetual questioning is all. What they have in common is the desire to wrestle with issues of free will and the existence of evil which help to define our humanity, as well as a conviction that there is more to our existence than 'getting and spending'.

When the last series was about to be broadcast I mentioned it to the highly intelligent barrister I was seated next to at dinner. Militantly atheistic, he scoffed at the whole idea and dismissed my agnosticism with contempt. When I mildly suggested that conviction in the non-existence of God is as big a leap of faith as born-again Christianity, since we cannot prove there is no God, he described my point as 'fatuous'. Irritated, I wondered why he was so emphatic. When a man doth protest that much, placing all his trust in science and logic, he should remember Freud: 'If one regards oneself as a sceptic, it is well from time to time to be sceptical about one's scepticism.'

I confess that a millennium visit to Jerusalem, a vile place most despicably polluted by competing 'faiths', all but pushed me into the 'anti' camp, and to be fair to that barrister, his rage against religion was fuelled by the events of 11 September 2001. Many people since have expressed to me the view that religion is, as it always has been, responsible for the great ills of the world. Two interviewees made reference to those terrible events. Pamela Stephenson, now practising in Los Angeles, spoke of the terror and helplessness felt by caregivers, from people like herself to rabbis and priests: 'people turning to them for answers when they didn't have any'. She went on: 'It was a chink in the universe, and there was no turning back.' For the best-selling international novelist Amy Tan, the message was not that all religion is harmful, but that Americans have to look at the way they have attempted to impose their beliefs on the rest of the world, and that nobody should attempt to impose their beliefs on anybody else. Of course; and how can one not but feel pity for the Christian God prayed to by racist, red-necked Bible-thumpers in the deep South, and for the Allah whose name is called by sick murderers? The great world faiths have been traduced by fundamentalism, corruption and political struggle, their essential philosophical strengths ignored. It's worth clinging to the thought that people divided by doctrine are united by the experience of love: the love of God (goodness), of one's neighbour, and the intense transforming love of family.

I no longer expect the dramatic conversion, the mystical fusion with the Holy Spirit; no tongues of flame or howling winds, no voice in the darkness or rending of the curtain. I still believe that the search for God is the quest for goodness, and that it can lead us through the valley of the shadow, not to an other-wordly Paradise but to an understanding of what it means to be human, and a desire to be *better*. I have knelt before the Buddha, wondered at the glory of a mosque, delighted in the tinselled cornucopia of a Hindu shrine, chanted to the goddess, wept as the names of the dead were spoken at a Greek Orthodox ceremony, and been rendered speechless by the felt presence of the Dreamtime Ancestors in the wild Australian Outback. I have visited holy places all over the world and see them as statements of the relationship between struggling humankind and its highest aspiration.

I am not the first to look with enchantment at my own life and gasp because it is all passing, changing, dying before my eyes: 'That which is only living can only die.' It is not the dread that this life is all, but that this *love* is all: the knowledge that one must look at this family calmly in the knowledge that 'one goodbye must be the last'. Will that be it? I think the answer is a blunt 'Yes', I doubt that the dead go on before us and we shall see them face to face, but . . . but . . . Upon the mere hint of a possibility many a soul has gone to the communion rail, many a weeping family found consolation in the shadow of the churchyard yew.

Still a devout sceptic, still questing, still believing in that goodness, I know these questions will go on being asked, the conversations continue, like the lighting of candles. The sense of the numinous links more people than one might think, in this secular, sex-obsessed and silly age – and it will go on taking me into churches, to meditate on the power of old stones, old faith, even when the organ is silent.

Kate Adie

Kate Adie began her broadcasting career in 1968 and
became the BBC's Chief News Correspondent in 1989,
covering most major international crises. She has won
eight major awards for her television journalism, was
awarded the OBE in 1993 and presents *From Our Own
Correspondent* on Radio 4.

*The essence of being a news reporter is to sum up a complex situation in
a few short and vivid sentences. Can you apply that skill to your own
relationship with religion?*

No, I can't. I've spent too long pondering at times of crisis and at
times when the emotion or the devastation or whatever is in front
of you – which is of great import – is happening, unable to come up
with what you can call spiritual answers. I'll give you a straight
example: I've sat through quite a lot of religious – 'addresses', shall
we call them? Sermons or speeches which occur, these days in
particular, after a great disaster. And there is usually some sort of
gathering in a church afterwards. And up comes usually an educated,
intelligent person, steeped in the law of his religion, and attempts
(and I can feel my feelings as I've sat in the back of those churches

or mosques or assembly halls: 'I can hear it coming . . .') to attempt to answer the question, 'Why has this happened?' And I've always sat through that and waited, almost like a hawk, for that moment. About two-thirds of the way through, having sympathised, talked about love and affection and care and sometimes the love of God, there comes this terrible moment when he's actually got to give the answer, 'Why?' What happens, I find, is that it moves into the realm of faith. You have to believe to follow him from that point. And that's when I've seen the congregation often fall away. It is this terrible business of explaining *why*. It leaves me, the reporter – and this is nothing actually to do with the reporting I'll be doing on the story – endlessly wondering about a next world or an all-powerful being, and why on earth dreadful things – an earthquake or a terrorist bomb or a flood or a war or some sort of terrible accident – occur. I see a lot of people – and I'd include myself – in that point at which you are just unable to have a blind acceptance.

When you were a child, did you believe in the old man in the sky?

I had a wonderfully ecumenical upbringing, without anybody knowing it. I was christened Methodist, so I've got all the hymns and I love the music. I was then trotted off to a determinedly militant C. of E. school, then for some reason transferred to a Presbyterian Sunday school, while at the same time part of the family had 'gone Catholic' – and thereby hung a lot of silence! – and a lot of neighbours were orthodox Jewish. So I grew up seeing a lot of different buildings and a lot of different rituals, and that's what fascinated me. Why did some people have a table and some people have an altar? Why did some people have nothing at all? Why did some people stand up *then?* This is what a child wonders, always being told to stand up, kneel down, sit, be quiet, read that, say this. And you did it differently in all these different buildings. That's the first thing that ever I noticed, and I was fascinated by that, because it seemed to *matter* to people, these little differences.

As a child watching all the different rituals, did you think that the person they were for was the same person? Was the idea of God fleshed out?

No, I don't think so. I remember specifically from a very early age, I associated religion with kindness. The Methodist church I very first went to as a tiny baby, carried into the choir to sit and play under the pews – and then later on, I remember the kindness of people, a kind of warmth. I still associate that with the Methodism of my childhood. That was it: people were kind and friendly and warm and welcoming. It was not an austere religion. It was full of fun and great music. I then began to associate the Anglican church with buildings because we were taken to Durham Cathedral occasionally, and I've got a life-long adoration of wonderful buildings, particularly cathedrals. So I was fascinated by all the different forms. That's all stayed. I don't know about the personal meaning of God. I don't think, as a child, I ever sat and thought . . .

I had the rebellion, which I think you get around fourteen or fifteen – a questioning of everything. I also spent a strange time as a Sunday school teacher where I was finally floored by some eight-year-old. I was going to give them a lot of comparative religion, I thought. And I'd get these small faces saying things like 'What's an angel?' There was me, the self-confident sixteen-year-old, floored. I gave up. I did not have the answers. I wouldn't now.

You describe a process of being very broad-minded and loving the beauty of buildings. That's an external, an aesthetic, isn't it – to appreciate the buildings and to love the pomp and ceremony of ritual?

I'm aware of the comfort of religion, yes, and I've seen many people comforted by it in all kinds of countries in all sorts of religion: a structure, a set of deeds (that is, a ritual) is comforting to people. And what underpins that is often certainties which are delivered on a plate by the ruling power of that religion, and a lot of people like that. They like their minds made up for them. So I'd only go so far, because I suppose what lies deep within me is a feeling that we have to take our own decisions. We bear our own responsibilities for our actions – very much so; and you cannot read it in a book or be told it by a cleric. You have to take responsibility yourself.

I have a rooted dislike of all extreme fundamentalist aspects of all religions. I've seen it kill so many people. I've seen it make people's lives a hell on earth. The moment you start moving along the fundamentalist road, in whatever religion, you begin destroying the human spirit and you take away responsibility. People don't become responsible for their own actions. They absolve it all to something else. You know: 'It's God's will.' The number of people who must have killed having lumped the responsibility on to a deity is frightening. That is when you really actually feel fear on a battlefield or in a war – when you see people who are about to try and kill you because they have the light of God in their eyeballs. That is really frightening.

The light of fanaticism – substituting fanaticism for God? But, defending God, people would say, 'Is it fair to lay that blame at God's door?'

I don't know, because I don't have a definition of everyone's God. I have a dilemma: I would love to feel that there was a supporting, wonderful, warm and good guiding principle, but I don't know at what point it seems to fall over the edge into the creature with the flaming sword, which puts others to the sword in the name of some deity. I think that comes down to another thing I suppose I'm guilty of: none of us reads theology these days. There's almost no knowledge of it as a subject. It's not even a hobby to people as it was in Victorian times, where it was an interest which educated people had. Few of us have theological arguments to back up our feelings and our groping towards what we feel about right and wrong, good and bad, and life and death.

Do you think that the knowledge would help people?

I think so, because most things have been argued before . . . There's nothing much new on the face of the earth in that way. People have been pondering – Neanderthal man must have stared up at the moon and wondered why it disappeared and the great globe of the sun came round the next morning. So people must have been wondering. People must have been thinking. And all the most basic thoughts about life eventually lead you to some sort of question about 'Why?' and 'Is there a greater power?' and all of these things. It has been argued for thousands of years by some of the greatest minds.

When you look up at the moon, is it that kind of moment when you – to all intents and purposes worldly, worldly-wise, experienced, tough maybe – is it at moments like that that you have a sense of the Other?

I'm not sure. I'm not sure at what points they occur. I do think the world is wonderful. There's so much to think about. I suppose with me, like everyone else, it comes down to the much more personal moments rather than those great long sights into the universe. It's much more personal. It comes down to death, our own mortality. When you consider that we are but a little speck and we have a short span of time: those matters are when you are brought up short yourself. I think, like a lot of people, I avoid – hop round – the subject.

I've seen a lot of people buried, in my job. I'm very aware that the body – wondrous as it is, complex – is but a body, and when you've seen it bulldozed into a mass grave, when you've seen it blown apart, when you've seen it desecrated, then I suppose I say to myself, 'It's just a body.' What was there was more important: the person, the personality, the character, and the collection of deeds and feelings and thoughts. A body is a body. It's a very sobering sight.

A body is a body, but do you believe in the soul?

I find it a difficult word. I cannot quite come to terms with the description of soul. I'm not quite sure what it is. I've seen one or two instances where I have been conscious that there is something moving that is greater. I have seen people *in extremis* do things which really everything on the material side of life doesn't warrant – there is *extra* in people, there are resources in people. If you talk to people or listen to people who have been tortured – if you listen to people who have lost everything – and they are still going on with life, often with extraordinary resources of generosity, kindness and no bitterness, there has to be something which motivates that more than just their experience of life and their character.

I once saw something very strange, and if anyone has the answer to this one . . . I used to live in northern Sweden, up by the reindeer. And I was in a village where a man was brought in after a dreadful farming accident. Most of his forearm was severed to the bone – the skin was lying off either side – and he was just pumping blood. A phone call was made by this extremely modern and extremely progressive Swedish family who lived in this remote area, to the hospital for an ambulance. And a second phone call was made. Within a couple of minutes a neighbour bicycled over – a middle-aged woman wearing a little neat hat and a grey coat, a little black handbag; she got off her bicycle, put the bicycle by the wall, walked into the kitchen, stood there, said 'Good afternoon' to everybody and stood in the corner of the room looking at this man, who was not far from – possibly – dying, and muttered. And I stood there. He was unconscious. The blood congealed on his arm. Just like that. She was a 'blood stopper'. I remember the feeling! I couldn't believe my eyes! Since then I've looked into it. I've been fascinated by the psychosomatic, by miracles, by all of these things. I've never found the answer to that one.

That was a miracle?

I don't like the word and never have done. She certainly didn't do it for spiritual reasons, either. It was just a gift. They don't talk about God with it. She wasn't a religious person. Now, ever since, I have always just said to myself, 'There are more things than we know about.' There may be a scientific answer. Maybe in another century we'll find an easy scientific answer to that one, because there were many things that puzzled people in the preceding centuries which, we now know, have straightforward scientific answers. I saw that one, and I don't know from what it flows.

On the other hand, I am deeply sceptical of so much that is trotted out as a miracle due to people's lack of understanding of theology. The time I was in northern Sweden, I was studying a group from what you would say was a fundamentalist or rather narrow nonconformist sect which went in for speaking in tongues and a certain amount of self-denial – a typical nineteenth-century Protestant sect. All of their so-called miracles are straightforwardly explained by twentieth-century science. So I have both sides: one side sceptical and one side with wonder. I'm a typical journalist: I sit on the fence between the two!

A typical devout sceptic! You talked about having seen lots of funerals – the pomp as well as people being shovelled unceremoniously into a mass grave. Do you think that's it? Do you have any sense at all of a life after death?

I've interviewed a lot of people who've talked about it. It may be. Again, I don't have a decision on it. It depends how you see death. A rather small scene comes to mind which had an effect on me. I'm still trying to work out why. After the Armenian earthquake there were bodies left lying around – a great number didn't get buried, really, because so many died and were just exposed or lying under rubble for weeks and months. In the midst of all of that, I followed a family one day up to a graveyard – and I'd never seen an Armenian Orthodox Christian burial, I know little about Armenian religion. But we followed them to this graveyard. And I felt, 'We're intruding. Here we are with a television camera.' They didn't seem to worry. It was a big family. They had lots of picnic baskets. The grave was already there and I found out later that they bury without ceremony: popped into the ground, nice and hygienic, soil over it, that's it. Then, after a lot of preparation, the family goes along. And they sat round the grave and they spread out their picnic tablecloths and they produced bottles and bottles of wine and brandy; a huge great – what they call a 'mourning cake', chocolate mourning cake with a big chocolate cross on it. Huge cake. Marvellous. All the contents of their larders – what they could find or scavenge, which wasn't a lot after that earthquake. They sat round. What they do is talk about him, and natter away and remember the good things. Somebody gets up and makes a speech. By that time they've all had a fair bit to drink and everybody's saying, 'He's a great guy! Do you remember when he did this? Do you remember that? Marvellous! Do you remember when you did this . . . ?' The whole family is brought into it. At the end, somebody gets up, makes a toast, they drink, and then the rest of the contents of the glass are thrown on to the grave for him to drink. And they pack up their baskets and very casually walk away. And they turned round and they *waved*.

There was something about that that gave me a sense of where we are on this earth. I don't know what it is. I found it one of the most moving things I've ever seen.

Are you ready to die?

No. I love life so much. I've seen a lot of people die. I love life so much. There's so much to do, to see, to feel, to hear, to love. I just find life exciting. I'll bore on this subject. I'll wake up in the morning and I think, like everybody else, 'God! I feel terrible.' But on other occasions I think, 'Think of the lucky things in my life! The wonderful things!' You count your blessings – now there's a phrase which I believe in very much. You count your blessings. I have been so lucky. There's so many wonderful things to do, to see . . .

Do you think the effect of the contemplation of death in you has been to make you love life more?

Yes, oh yes.

And value it . . . ?

Yes. When you see how death snatches people away, robs families, cuts people short – all those phrases which are used in our language are all true. I've been in a crowd where people have been shot. Why not me? There but for the grace of God.

That phrase, too – full of meaning – slips very easily off the tongue. Do you believe in grace?

Why should I have it and no one else? Or do other people not have it? That's what I can't understand. That comes back again to the faith. Why are some graced in life? Some people call it luck. Some people call it blessing. Why do some people get it and not others, when you can't see in a logical way, evaluating these people's lives? Why are some people cut short?

I'm no profound thinker, but as a journalist you spend a lot of time listening to people. You have to listen to people, for example, who lose a child. This is something where you cannot come away from listening to people talking this through without a sort of yawning chasm in front of you saying, 'Why? Why?' Contemplating these matters, I don't find it entirely comforting at times – you know, to look at the size of the universe and the complexity of this wonderful earth. There are times when there seems to be a large black hole, and some people have fallen into it.

If I could offer you absolute proof, now, that God existed, would you be glad?

I'd be puzzled . . . Because I would have thought that the revelation should have come at the dawn of time and continued onwards. I would have thought it a bit of a game if we only found out now. But that apart . . . I remember reading quite a lot on the subject of faith, the point of faith. This is where logic, scientific knowledge, self-knowledge, an understanding of how society works, of how human beings function, all come along to this very point at which faith has to take over. It happens in all major religions. It's a fascinating point, and I am stood there at that point. Wondering.

(1995 conversation)

Isabel Allende

Isabel Allende was born in Peru in 1942 and achieved international fame in 1982 with her first novel, *The House of the Spirits*. This was followed by (among others) *Of Love and Shadows* (1984), *The Infinite Plan* (1991), *Daughter of Fortune* (1999) and *Portrait in Sepia* (2000). In 1994 she published *Paula* as a memoir for her daughter, and her writing has received many awards world-wide.

I was brought up in a very Catholic, conservative, patriarchal environment. My grandmother, however, was always fascinated with the spirit world and she had seances, which were forbidden by the Church. And so there was this part of our life which was strict, conventional Catholicism, and the other part that was the wildness of my grandmother's imagination. And both things were sort of combined, but then my grandmother died when I was very young, and the house was a house of mourning. My grandfather painted the furniture black. Desserts, flowers, parties, music, the radio – everything was forbidden. As I was growing up, I felt the weight of Catholicism. There was the beauty of the ritual, the beauty of Christmas and the beauty of the church, but also the heaviness of sin and guilt.

How did you respond, as a little girl, to the image of Christ on the cross?

Terribly. I still do. I have a Christ there on my table, and last night I had a dream about Christ and the cross. It's very hard for me to imagine a tortured man on a cross as a symbol of faith and life and love. I did not understand the reason. I did not understand why Christ had died – and I still don't. I lost my faith. I did not believe that anything of what I was being told was true. I did not believe that Christianity was the only way that you could be good, or go to heaven, or whatever. I did not believe that Christ was the son of God who had died on the cross for my sins. I did not believe in a god that was like a punishing judge, that was so unforgiving.

Did you talk to anybody about these doubts?

No, I just walked out of the Church. At the time, I also became a feminist. I was a leftist. I became involved in politics – not actively, but I started thinking about politics. I started reading. The more I read, the more I walked away from the Church, and from patriarchy, and then from male chauvinism. I started reading feminist writers and I realised that I had this anger in me that I couldn't manifest. And then I found an articulate language to express all that. But I couldn't talk about this with my mother. She was too busy doing other things. She was in a survival state . . . she had been excommunicated because she fell in love with a married man. So although she believed and she had the need of the Church, she was not allowed in the Church. In a way, I resented that very much, too. Although I didn't believe in the Church, I resented the fact that my mother had been expelled. Very angry, because I always saw the Church as the epitome of patriarchy, like the military.

I had been brought up with the idea that everything bad you do, you pay for. And it was very clear what was bad and what was not bad. But when I walked away from the Church, then I questioned everything. I started questioning what was considered bad and what was considered good, and I realised that many of the bad things were very good, actually. And I wanted not only to do them, but to export them if possible. So I became very subversive, rebellious; I started studying philosophy, reading philosophy. Then I started looking for other religions. I turned to Buddhism . . . that was later in my life, though. I started studying to see what other religions had to offer, and they are all very similar. Buddhism is not really a religion, it's a way of life. But it is also very patriarchal. So I couldn't find anything that would fit me, or suit me.

My mother said something really smart once. She said, 'Well, religions are not designer-made. They're not made for you.' And I said, 'Well, this is a club, and I don't like the rules of this club, and I don't want to belong in this club.' So we had a lot of confrontation then, when I was growing up. And now my mother is eighty-one and I will be sixty this year, and I think we are much closer in that sense. My mother has gone back to being a Catholic. She's back in the Church. I have become more tolerant because I understand that these are all manifestations of the same need, and probably the same god . . .

There was a period in my life, between twenty-five and forty-five, when women . . . all my friends were questioning everything, and moving away from whatever religious backgrounds they had had. Then, when my daughter Paula died – I was fifty – I found a group of women, older women, who became my spiritual sisters. And so we invented a sort of spiritual practice that has replaced the rituals of the Church.

What sort of rituals?

For example, we will get together every week and we pray, but we don't pray as I was taught to pray, repeating words like mantras. No, we get together; we share our lives – and this is not group therapy! But just by sharing our lives and being witness of the life of another woman, we learn a lot. And then we put on the table the names of the people who are in need. Sometimes it's people we know who are either sick or going through some hardship; or sometimes it's just the world. For example, the Middle East, or the women in Afghanistan, the children in Pakistan – that kind of thing. And then we meditate and send all our energy to heal and to connect.

Do you believe in that power of visualisation?

I think there is some energy that we have; we don't know how it works. Before humanity could learn about electricity and discover the rules of electricity, we would see what electricity did, but we didn't know how. We would see the effect and not know the cause. And I see there is an effect of positive thinking, and there is an effect of negative thinking – you get sick. If you start carrying around a load of negative energy, you end up sick. The Dalai Lama is the best example of positive energy, and the healing power of positive energy. So I do believe that if a group of people get together and send to the world this kind of healing force, this light, it might do good.

Yes, I do believe in little miracles and in big miracles, but mainly in little ones. And I do believe in signs.

Can you give me an example?

I can give you several, but I will give you the most recent one. You know, Paula's husband, Ernesto – he's like my son and he calls me Mother, and we really love each other dearly. And after many years of being a widower and being very sad, he found a wonderful young woman and married her. She's called Julia. Julia was born the same day that Paula was born. Her mother is called Paula. Her father was born the same day – and we're talking the same *year* – I was born. After a year or so, they decided they wanted to start a family, and they wanted to come closer to us. But of course it was very difficult, because they were living in New York and he had a job. He sent a thousand résumés all over the country, and he got a senior position ten minutes away from this house. He's going to move into my old house, where Paula died, and the day that he's moving is the same day that we brought Paula from the hospital to that house, where she eventually died. And this is not planned. This just happened. So when you see all these dates and these coincidences, these are little miracles.

One of your novels is called The Infinite Plan. *I'm wondering if you have any sense that all that set of wonderful coincidences is God-given?*

I don't believe in God as I was taught, but I do believe that maybe there is some kind of incredible network, a connection, a sort of spider web, or many spider webs that connect things, places, events. I think that everything has cause and effect, that we don't live long enough to see the relationship between events and the connections. But they are there, and they are magical. I believe that everything I do, even the bad thoughts – or the good thoughts – comes back somehow.

Your book Paula *is a long meditation on Paula's death. She fell into a coma in 1991 and was in hospital in Spain for a long time until you bought her home to California. In that book, you turn again and again to the contrast between your mother's Catholic faith – that faith was also shared by Paula, a very devout and ascetic young woman – and your own belief in what you call 'the goddess'. I'd like to explore that.*

I mean that if there is any human form of God, in any way, it should be feminine. It's nurturing, healing, it is someone that holds you in the womb. It's not someone who goes to war, who punishes, who judges, who decides anything; it's Mother Earth, it's whatever is nurturing.

When we were in the hospital in Madrid, the only quiet, silent, lonely place in that huge hospital was the chapel. It was always empty. We would go there with my mother, because it was a place where nobody smoked and we could be alone. And while my mother would kneel down and pray to this image of Christ on the cross, I would look at the Virgin Mary, who was holding a child. And I was thinking, 'Please, please, if there is a goddess out there, hold my child. Just wrap my child in your tunic or your arms or whatever, and keep her safe from pain.' I didn't pray so much for a miracle as for what I would do with a newborn baby: just keep the baby warm, feed the baby.

Did you ever feel a response?

No. I never did, until Paula died. When she died, there was a little sign that was very significant. Paula died on 6 December, a Saturday; and the next Tuesday I got together with my prayer group. We are six women. We got together, and because it was going to be Christmas we had new candles for the meeting. And we had the candles around the little circle, and I had been crying, and one of the people in the group said, 'What do you *want*, Isabel?' And I said, 'A sign. I just need a sign.' And she said, 'How do you feel?' And I said, 'I feel this burning presence in my womb – something that is burning like a flame in my womb.'

So we held hands for a while and then we closed our eyes and we started our meditation, sending prayers up there. And all of a sudden I heard the voice of one of my friends, who said, 'Let's have a look at your candle.' And I looked at my candle, and it was burning in the middle, and it had a sort of cavity in the womb of the candle as if it was burning in the womb. My first reaction was, 'It is a defective candle.' And surely it was. But why did it start burning in the centre at that very moment? Why was it my candle and not anybody else's candle?

So I have kept that candle. I always have it with me, and when I need a sign I remember the candle and I say, 'There are signs.' We have to surrender to the fact that they do exist and be aware. Listen to the voices, see the little miracles, because we live in a hurry, so busy and so worried that we don't stop. And at that moment when I stopped, I saw the sign that I hadn't seen during all that year when Paula was sick, because I was just out of my mind, I was crazy with grief.

And did you take the sign as meaning that Paula's spirit was with you and would always be with you?

Yes. The spirit had a journey, and the spirit would do whatever journey it had to do. But there was something as strong as the spirit, and that was the memory of her that I could have inside me, and she would be with me in many ways.

When Paula was in hospital and you were using all the power you had to ask the Virgin, the goddess, whomsoever, to look after her as best they could – having rejected the God of your childhood, who did you blame, what did you blame?

The doctors. I didn't blame God, and I didn't think that my case was special in any way. Why would my child live? Other children die all the time. The oldest sorrow of humanity is children dying, and mothers have had to live with that since the beginning of all time. Why would it not happen to me? Am I so special that my children will live longer than I? I don't know. I don't think so.

So you concentrated on what you saw as human error.

It was malpractice. So I concentrated on saving Paula's body from that place and those people, and hoping that I could move some resources to heal her. I didn't know how serious her condition was. They never told me that she had severe brain damage and that she was in a vegetative state. I learned that later. But at the time, I just blamed the doctors. I never blamed God. I never thought Paula had been punished or I had been punished . . .

I don't think that the universe is particularly benevolent. I think that the universe just is, and we are part of it, and there are some natural laws. We all die. We all deteriorate. Everything changes. Everything happens fast and everything goes away. And the more we get attached to things, the more we suffer. I believe in all those things.

But in the book Paula, *there's a wonderful passage where you describe the Andes and a journey you made. And it was an epiphany in your life where you seemed to see God – using 'God' very loosely – in that landscape.*

I see the divine everywhere, which is different from God. I see the divine nature of everything that exists. When Paula was sick, I would run in the woods and cry, and it was winter and I would get all wet with rain and just crawl in the mud and scream. And I felt the divine in the mud, in the trees, in nature, in the connections that people made with me, the letters I got, the connection with my mother. My mother was with me for a hundred days until she collapsed. And then we corresponded. She went back to Chile, and I would write sometimes two or three letters a day to my mother. And that very strong connection has a divine energy in it.

Then I realised there was something divine also in the state in which my daughter was. My daughter was not my daughter any more. What was that thing in that bed? She couldn't move. She was totally paralysed. I would stare for hours at her black eyes and see nothing. There was no recognition of any kind. She had to be fed through a tube in the stomach. The only thing that she could do by herself was breathe. Nothing else. So her body started to deteriorate to a point that maybe she would not have been recognised by her friends. Her grace was gone, her voice, her goodness, everything, as she became this creature in this bed. When her body changed and her mind went, she was still there. Who was she? What was there in that room? Her spirit. There was something there that left when she died, but it was there all the time.

So I felt that she was doing something, that there was a reason why she stayed trapped in that body. And the reason was not only that I kept her alive artificially. There was a reason why she was there, until she decided at some point that she needed to go. And I remember exactly how that happened. Because by the end of November, nothing had apparently changed, but I felt that she was leaving. I felt it so strongly that I called Ernesto in New York, where he was living, and I said, 'Ernesto, something is changing. I can't tell you what, but something is changing. Come.' And Ernesto came to California. He said, 'I don't see what you see. I see her exactly as I saw her a few weeks ago. But if you believe this, I think that you are the mother and you know.' And I said, 'I think that she's trapped because we don't let her go.' And so he and I went to the room where she was and we locked the door and we held her in our arms, and we told her that she could go. And she did – six days later. So, she couldn't understand anything, but her spirit somehow got it.

Her spirit heard you.

I think she did, yes.

You asked rhetorically why it was happening. Why did it happen?

Paula was a teacher. She was a teacher in normal life. That was her job. When she was little, she loved to play teacher, play school with the dolls. And I think that I wasn't ready, Ernesto wasn't ready, to let her go. And we had a lot to learn – especially me. And I think she stayed to teach me a few things.

She taught me to be detached. She taught me that the only thing that one has is what one gives away. By spending oneself, one becomes rich. And once you've thrown overboard everything, there's one thing left: the only thing left is the love you've given or the love you give. That was probably the most important lesson in my life. It took away all the fears. I am not afraid of death. I am not afraid of failure, of loneliness, of old age, of almost nothing. I am afraid, of course, of violence, and I don't want my grandchildren or my son to suffer. But aside from that, I have a very wonderful life, a very happy life, because I've learned to let go. And I would have never learned that without Paula teaching that to me. I don't control anything, and it's a wonderful feeling when you realise that you have no power. You do your best with the knowledge you have, and that's it.

So you've moved a long way from that rigid Catholicism of your childhood.

Yes, I've moved a long, long way. On the other hand, now I see it with different eyes. Now I see the meaning more than the form. Before, I rejected so much – the richness of the Church, the wealth, and the poverty of the poor. The contrast between these old, celibate men who were instructing poor women in the world about contraception, for example. How dare they? All those things were the form. But there's more than that. There is the message of Christ. There is the fact that so many people who believe in whatever they believe do good.

What to you is the most essential thing about the message of Christ?

Forgiveness, I think. It is the fact that we can forgive almost everything. At an individual level, in a personal level in our lives, we can forgive. And when we forgive we sort of get rid of something that is so heavy. I remember that for a long time I felt that I could never forgive the torturers in Chile – people who would torture children in front of their parents; that I could never forgive the doctors that ruined my daughter's life. And now I realise that I can, of course I can.

Who am I, first of all, to judge anybody? And then, who knows if, in the same circumstances, I would do the same thing? Potentially we're all alike. If someone can be Mother Teresa, so can I. And if someone can torture, so can I, given the wrong circumstances. So whatever any human being can do, I can do too. And if there are people who can torture, probably, given the wrong circumstances, I would do the same. And if there's people like Mother Teresa, maybe I can do that too. I feel that potentially we are all alike, and we have different destinies and different circumstances. Some of us are very lucky: we never have to do something like that. We were never so afraid, so screwed up, that we ended up torturing somebody.

And is this also part of the lesson of suffering?

It is part of the lesson of suffering, but it is also the lesson of joy, of all the wonderful things that we have in life. My life has been about losses and about separation, abandonment, grief; but also about a lot of love and joy and success and books and children and dogs . . . and chocolate! Great things. I learn from all of that.

I wouldn't talk about consolation because it's more, or it's beyond that: it's a positive, radiant acceptance of the world as is, with the bad and the good, and the fact that I have this energy to change what I don't like. And I may not see the change in my lifetime, but anything that I do today will have an effect sooner or later, and maybe my great-great grandchildren will see the effect of my work – as I have lived in *my* life the effect of the work of so many people who did good before I came to this world. I would not be a feminist today or a writer today if other people hadn't thought those ideas before, and fought, and maybe sometimes sacrificed their lives for those causes that today make my life easier. So that's why I feel that everything I do has an effect on the world, and I feel empowered, and I feel this energy that is not wasted and is not passive. And it's not about suffering. It's about doing positive good things – with a tremendous hope that it has an effect.

(2002 conversation)

Simon Russell Beale

Simon Russell Beale is widely considered one of the finest actors of his generation. Born in 1961, he gained a first in English at Cambridge University, trained at the Guildhall, and has been an Associate Artist of the Royal Shakespeare Company and a member of the Royal National Theatre. Among many roles on stage and screen, his Hamlet (2000) was a triumph and gained him two prestigious awards.

If you were to act the part of God, how would you play him?

Certainly not as the God of Our Fathers, the Old Testament God. I've always had a sort of feeling that God, with any luck, is more humane than we are, and most of the people I know are very humane and non-judgmental people. So I suppose if I were to act my ideal of God . . . then it would be somebody just very nice and very forgiving.

You've played a lot of bad people, wicked people, and I half-expected you to perhaps see God as someone who was quite vengeful.

In all the great plays they do suffer for it; then I suppose the suffering would allow God to forgive you and I suppose that's the ideal pattern. If you're brought up in the Church of England, as I was, then you get a lot of judgments thrown at you. I suppose I just can't believe that God would want to destroy his own creation or to judge his own creation too harshly. If you play a part like Richard III – he's not a nice man – then I think you get an understanding of the sheer black misery of being evil, and that's its own punishment. Perhaps that's too simple – I don't know. But the idea of an outside force coming in and sort of whopping you on the head for being evil, or when you've probably gone through the agonies of being evil, I find a bit harsh. I do realise there are people who have no sense of a moral code and are therefore not aware of their evil. I suppose that's the definition of being a psychopath, isn't it? But for the majority of people, if they do evil or do an evil act then I suspect it carries its own punishment with it. That's the economic system – whereas the less economic system is to live an afterlife and get thrown into eternal damnation.

You've raised the ideas of good, evil and an afterlife. Does that mean that you would count yourself as a believer? Or why do you identify with the title of this series?

Well, I think it is fear. I'd love to be able to alchemise it into hope, which I suppose is what happens when you finally decide or when it's revealed to you that you have a faith. At the moment I don't have a faith, so therefore I'm just simply frightened that I'm missing out on something that's blatantly obvious to the people who do have a faith.

Was this always your position when you were a child, or were you a believer?

I went to a choir school and I was brought up in a family that attended church; I went to a church service every day of my life until I was twenty-two. I was a choral scholar and inevitably – especially between about seven and thirteen – I just assumed I believed. When I got confirmed I assumed that I believed everything that was being told me. I mean, imagine: every single day, for at least four hours a day, you were singing something religious, and for an hour a day at least you were actually praising God. I remember when we had a bomb scare at St Paul's Cathedral: I remember the Dean was rather magnificent and he came down and all the choir were sitting there thinking he was going to cancel Evensong and he said, 'Absolutely not. We are going forward and we will continue to praise God in a ceaseless round of praise. We did it during the Second World War and we're not going to let some little bomb scare put us off.' Thrilling, of course.

And then at university or during the late years of school, I suppose you suddenly start all the questioning. I just suddenly thought, 'There are holes in this argument and I don't have the wherewithal to cover them up or fill them in.' Things just didn't seem to be economical. And I kept on thinking, 'Surely he or she might have been able to get a system that was a little more efficient, if he wanted his creation to be good?'

The problem of pain?

The problem of why people go through pain. If you want people to strengthen and if you want people to grow, then surely there must have been some system we don't know of or that we can't understand, that doesn't involve such pain.

On the other hand you could say that in many cases pain is a source of growth.

That's always what's said. I mean, I've never suffered pain like a lot of people have, not in any way, so I don't know what the feeling is like, of growing through pain to a greater strength. And there must surely be failures, that's the other thing. There must surely be people who suffer enormous pain and become embittered; I don't know. I think the response of the human mind isn't that predictable, so therefore why did he choose that way to strengthen us?

So you wanted the universe to be benign – perhaps a political wish on your part? You want good to prevail, and equality, and when it doesn't you think there can't be a god because you don't want the idea of God to be the person who allows that to happen?

Yes. God is a sort of trickster. God is a person who tests us, and that I find really hard.

You spent all that time between the ages of seven and twenty-one singing in religious services. Does the language of the liturgy, of the Book of Common Prayer, of the Authorised Version of the Bible, still have a relevance for you?

One of the props in the play that I'm doing at the moment is the Book of Common Prayer, a most beautiful edition, and I picked up, 'Lighten our darkness, we beseech thee, O Lord', the great collect at the end of Evensong . . . I worry myself slightly sometimes when I get excited by that – it still summons up an enormous amount of memories of Evensong at St Paul's.

And does it sum up what is essentially a human need?

I think I'm usually quite a happy person, but I went through a bad patch about two years ago, and before I went to sleep I used to say that prayer again and again, making it singular instead of plural, 'Lighten my darkness, I beseech you, O Lord.' Yes, so therefore there must be something in me that wanted to say that. It's such a wonderful phrase, 'Lighten our darkness', such a wonderful idea. It's the answer to everything, really. Just lighten my darkness.

Your repetition of it must have implied a belief that it's possible.

It's possible – yes, absolutely. So this is the devout part of the title. I don't know where the lightening of the darkness would come from, but just that it's possible.

Would it be true to say that you can sympathise with the need for a personal God but have problems with the organisation of that need – the Church itself?

In a nutshell – yes. Even if I don't trust in a personal God I do trust in a fount of good, a source of good or a centre of good. But we do have problems with the presentation of it by the Church. And it's not simply that I think it's all nonsense – I certainly don't think that . . .

Have you explored other religions?

No. In order to get some sort of perspective I suppose I should. But no. I suppose if I was to be absolutely honest, if I were to have a faith, I guarantee I'd end up in the Church of England – probably.

So what's your problem? If I was the Archbishop of Canterbury and you could say to me. 'Look, this is what I want put right,' can you sum it up?

Well, the big one is that I don't know whether or not I believe that God sent down his son.

Lots of bishops don't know that either . . .

Yes, it's a really tricky one, that. It doesn't worry me that there's not necessarily a virgin birth . . . although I think it's essential to agree with the resurrection. I think the really fundamental thing for me is that I would have to believe that God took the effort to send his son, and I can't do that. There are other reasons why I find the teachings on personal morality and the Church tricky, but I think those are obviously less important than that fundamental. You've got to believe in your Creed, haven't you? . . . I can't.

You don't have a problem believing there was this prophet Jesus? This historical figure who did good? You have no problem with that? You said you want to believe that God made the 'effort' to send his son . . . you want to believe that he was that good, that humane?

Yes, that personal, I suppose. It is easy enough to believe that there's a sort of source of good, a personal source of good, but it's trickier to believe that there's somebody who bothered enough to send a message through his son. I'm not quite sure what this son thing is.

If you require an answer to that question before agreeing to the Church, then of course you could never join the Church, because there can never be an answer, can there?

Faith, presumably, is a gift from somewhere, isn't it? Are you given the gift of faith? Are you given the grace?

I suppose that would be the evangelical interpretation, but there could be the other one – which is that faith can be an intellectual construct. Does that have any appeal to you? Or does it have to be a bolt from the blue?

I suppose I'm waiting for a bolt from the blue – but yes, I suppose as a second best . . . an alternative. The trouble is, that's like a Meccano construct, just missing one of the bolts, and you know you can have the most marvellous construction but missing just this tiny little bolt. Perhaps a lot of people find that last bolt difficult to put in, and perhaps most people who profess a Christian belief are probably much the same as me. Perhaps also it's laziness on my part because it does take commitment and effort. Perhaps I'm just waiting to summon up the energy.

Do you feel that asking all the questions that you do enables you to bring a bit extra to some of the great roles in the theatre?

I wouldn't presume to say that I bring a sense of spirituality because I don't think I've got it . . . I've had the luck to deal with the greatest playwriting in the history of the world and you can't do the end of

36

The Tempest, with that great surge of love and redemption, without somehow receiving comfort from it, relating it – at least relating it to yourself in some way.

When Lear is holding the dead Cordelia in his arms and asks, 'Why should a horse, a dog, a rat have life, and thou no breath at all?' it takes us back to that fundamental question, doesn't it? Do you come to the end of that play believing in the possibility of grace, or feeling a sort of rage that it all had to happen?

The part I was playing was Edgar – I suppose a symbol of grace and strength – and Robert Stevens was playing Lear, and that whole last section from when he wakes up out of madness was extraordinary. I'm contradicting myself a bit now, because there was unquestionably growth through the pain. Shakespeare somehow gets out of it, in that you don't quite know whether Lear's regained his former sanity, but equally well you could say that Lear is finding a new sanity that bears no relation to the sanity in the other acts. I never felt that it was an unredemptive end – even with the dead body of your daughter in your arms. It was a redemptive end.

Do you believe in the idea of grace in your own life?

Yes – I think. I don't mean in the sense of luck, success, but I'm loved and I love people so I suppose that's the biggest grace I can think of at the moment – as opposed to grace in the Church's terms. That will be the moment when I step through the gate into the fold – when I get that little bit of grace from God.

(1995 conversation)

Melvyn Bragg

Created a life peer in 1998, Lord Bragg is known variously as a power within arts television, an influential radio and television presenter, an academic and playwright, and a prolific and talented novelist. His works include *The Hired Man* (1969), *The Maid of Buttermere* (1987), *Credo* (1996) and *The Soldier's Return* (1999), which won the W.H. Smith Award.

To remember when I became aware of the idea of God is too difficult, really. I was very much aware of religion in an extremely specific way because I joined the choir at the local church when I was five or six. This was the time of World War II – I was born in 1939 – and most things were brought forward for children. I went to school when I was about three, like a lot of children then, so that my mother could work. They called for children for the choir and we sat on benches in front of the real choir stalls. They didn't have enough surplices so we just wore cassocks, none of which were the right length at all. I always liked singing so I was aware of hymns and psalms and listening to the sermons, although we were allowed to distract ourselves during the sermons. After I became too fidgety the vicar came to the house and said to my mother, 'If he's going to fidget like that he can bring a comic.' So I used to read these comics. But the idea of God, that developed later – somewhere around the age of nine or ten when you began to think of yourself as a particular human being . . . to define yourself and think, 'I am this sort of person, therefore I bear relation to this, that and the other.' So the idea of a God would have appeared later than going to church. Going to church was a quite extraordinary experience for me, certainly one of the biggest outside-the-house experiences of my childhood and early adolescence.

It was everything, really. There wasn't television – we listened to the radio – but in the church you were in the middle of this drama every week, dressing up, singing these wonderful words with these great melodies. This was a tiny town of five thousand people with eleven churches, and we had a sixty-strong choir at one stage. So you were in the middle of a tremendous sound . . .

There were the rituals in the church. There was the sermon. There were these magnificent words. And so it was a great spectacle and another, very special world, that had to be obeyed and somehow governed people's lives – but you couldn't work out why.

You paint this picture of this little boy caught up in a spectacle which sounds, as you describe it, very aesthetic, apart from anything else. Do you think that formed another side of you which was later to respond to the arts?

I think so. I think it formed a lot of me, partly because it was something that you didn't have to strive for. I honestly think that the deepest education you get is when you're not looking. You didn't go to church to learn but you learned massively. I can remember the words of innumerable hymns, scores of psalms – just imagine the effect it must have had on our minds, that at least twice a week, and more if you count the school assemblies in the mornings – and you were read good portions from the Bible, spoken in a very clear voice by the vicar or by a reader at school or a school teacher or whoever. So you got the rhythm of the King James' version, the complicated words, which were different from the way we use words nowadays so you had to make sense of the description of these characters, these battles and temptations, and the great triumphant story of Christ up to the crucifixion.

And so the music, the sound of the words, the words themselves, the participating in all that was going on, had a tremendous effect on anybody who entered into it and went through it, and I find that right across my generation . . .

At nine or ten or eleven, around that age, I was a complete and fervently devout Christian, you would say in a zealous way, thinking that there was one God, that there was a Trinity, believing literally in the New Testament. I suppose, if pressed, I'd have believed literally in Genesis.

Teenage is often a time when young people rebel against what you had to 'obey' – the religious community, the teachings of the Church and the choir practice and everything. Didn't you ever rebel against it?

Well, I went along with it. When I was about seventeen I started to have considerable doubts and had a rather bad time deciding that it was quite clearly stupid to believe in the literalism of the miracles. I now think I was a bit stupid, actually, but I thought *that* was stupid then. I thought you couldn't take seriously the idea of bringing someone alive from the dead, or even Christ himself coming back from the dead, and therefore what did that leave you with? If the resurrection wasn't true then where was Christianity? I had those doubts, but it didn't stop me keeping on going to church and, even in my first year at university, going to chapel, reading the lessons, being in the college choir. So in that sense I was a late faller-away rather than a late developer.

What caused the falling away?

I think it was an accretion of doubts, really, and an accumulation of other interests. Eighteen is about the only time in your life when you think you know everything. I don't say this entirely lightly. I think that's connected with the fact that most heroes in battle are around the age of eighteen, nineteen, twenty – that's the time when you've got through adolescence and you haven't become stained with adulthood, and you're poised there. I think you feel you're in a wonderful position where you can do what you want and nothing will be harmed. I think that propels people to rush into the rifle's mouth, and I think it also propels people to rush away from churches and institutions and rail against them.

I walked away. I didn't rail against it then because I had too much affection for it, and I felt it had given me such a lot and there was so much I liked about it. Oddly enough, it's turned itself inside out, really. What I liked about it then, when I was a late teenager, was its institutional forms. I liked going to services in cathedrals. I liked the forms: the singing, the processions, the psalms, the lessons, the form of the service. But I was worried about the core of it. I thought the core of it just didn't stand. Now, curiously enough, the institutional side of it seems to me to have, partly through its own fault – and I *do* think it's a fault – peeled and flaked away, whereas the core of it I'm much more interested in. The core of religion is something that I'm much more sympathetic to than I've ever been since I was blindly taken up with it when I was a kid.

Can you define that core?

It seems to me there are two or three things that matter in religion. One is to do with the beginning of things. The argument over the past few years particularly has been rehearsed to bits, but if you believe that there was a creator then you have to believe that there's a force out there, a guiding intelligence of a certain sort, out of which we all come. So far nobody has disproved that there is a creator. They get nearer and nearer the Big Bang but they never get there. And those who say it was God who started it seem to me to have as good a case as anybody. So that's one thing.

The second thing is that if you believe that there's a creator then you have to believe that what follows is designed by that creator – the argument from design which Paley, in the eighteenth century, famously went in for. And again, the more that's found out, the more you see objects of extraordinary apparent differences. Asteroids and eggshells are intimately related to each other: how they're structured, how they're formed. All these things have a deep and profound similarity, and that would accord with a religious idea.

And then, third – and this is a difficult one, I think – not only is there a creator and a design but there is a creator who has a design on us, on humankind, and his design is to give us free will in order that we can eventually achieve a moral perfection. The he or she or it will send messages through people. One of these people is Christ, another might have been Mohammed, and so it goes on. That's the hardest one to accept. It does seem to me, though, that occasionally coming into the planet – rather like that asteroid which killed off the dinosaurs sixty-five million years ago – are certain people so radically different in what they say that they do seem to bring messages. Do you think that Christ was just another man, but of a particularly heightened sense, who was taken out for a mixture of reasons to do with local politics and local zealotry and local passions and nothing to do with the central core? Or do you think he was someone who brought a new way of thinking to the world, a salvation to the world? If so, why did he bring that, what was propelling him, what was in him to do that? That's where it gets really interesting . . .

When you think about it, what Christ said two thousand years ago is extraordinarily radical. He came to a warrior society where might was right. In most parts of the world it was still an eye for an eye and a tooth for a tooth. And he said the most extraordinary things. He said, 'Blessed are the meek.' What was he talking about? 'Blessed are the poor.' Who does he think he is? 'Turn the other cheek.' At that time these were absurd ideas, and yet they're about the only ideas that make sense if a lot of people are going to live together on an increasingly crowded planet with diminishing resources. It's a profound sense. It's a newness. You wonder where that comes from. So that's the third step – but it interests me very much at the moment and will continue to interest me . . .

Moving on now, do you think it's true to say that religion is sneered at among people who you would consider your peers?

I don't think so. I think that people are effectively indifferent to it, mostly. And a fair-sized minority of people are quite thoughtful about it but tend to keep it to themselves, because it's such a difficult, big subject and lends itself to easy generalisations. What is life? Is there a future? Will we live after death? So first of all I think religion worries people because it brings up big, 'easy' questions and must be more difficult than that. Second, I think religion has played such a massive part in our intellectual, artistic and social history we don't quite know what to do with it, so it's an embarrassment in that sense. And then, third, there are stirrings, especially from the world of science, which are reviving ideas which have been dormant for a long time, particularly the idea of the origin of things and the idea of the association from one thing to another, the patterning . . .

The genetics notion at the moment is 'Can we change ourselves? Can we make ourselves different?' which is now a real possibility. Can we just take out this gene for this and that? Well, we can. There's also the beguiling idea of the future. I don't suppose anybody listening to this programme will not have had an experience – and quite a powerful experience – of feeling the presence of somebody they've lost and thought very strongly about. Now we know that people linger in our genes – I am my father and his father and my mother and her mother, and so it goes on, right back at least nine thousand years to Cheddar Man and obviously well before then.

But what is this lingering? Is it that there are essences and presences which do linger, as many serious cultures believe, including our own, for a very long time? That's what All Souls' Night is about. Now I think this is coming into consciousness. Now it's all getting mixed up with the rubbish of *The X-Files* and the excesses of science fiction and the crudities of Hollywood. But inside that, it seems to me, there's a melting pot of ideas which are leading a lot of people back to thoughts about religion, whether or not it's making them religious. And then finally, it seems that as a society we have actually got to work out codes of conduct, and religion did that for us. How we live in our society. What the moral laws are and what's the authority for moral laws. Is it the state? We don't trust the state very much in this country, thank goodness. Is it the Church? But that brings us back to religion, because religion brought moral authority. So, for all these reasons, people are thinking about it again.

And asking questions. But in the end, doesn't there come a point where the questions have to stop and the issue of faith arises?

Yes, faith is an acceptance, and I have moments of tremendous faith and don't know what to do with them. They don't occur at regular times. You read in literature of moments of being 'surprised by joy'. You feel it sometimes when you hear music. You think, 'Oh, *that's* what the world's like.' Or you hear a few lines from Shakespeare when you're in the right mood and you think, 'Oh, *that's* what it's like.' Those are things that need to be thought about harder and pursued, as, of course, people did for centuries before this.

You wrote a personal article a while ago about having, over a number of years as a boy, terrifying out-of-body experiences. Do you believe in the soul, then, as something distinct from, although lodged in, the body?

If I were asked that question on pain of life and death, I would say, yes, I do. It's an impossible question to answer, for obvious reasons, in that it doesn't stand up to any proof you can think of, but from the experiences I had it is possible for some essential thing in you, the thinking . . . to be removed from this corporeal frame, as it's been described, and exist somewhere else, in my case in the corner of a room. After I'd written that article I got a great number of letters from people saying they had floated around the town where they were born, in cities, across the seas . . . One of the things which interests me about the description of out-of-body experiences, where people have almost died and floated towards death and pulled back, is that they're always the same . . . Early Christian writing is full of such descriptions. So in terms of evidence, what does it add up to? It adds up to the possibility of continuity, the notion that there may be something so distinctive and extraordinary, something that does exist outside what we are, what we seem to be. If I had strong faith I'd say it is a fact. It's something that has to be grappled with, because if you're going to believe in a patterning and creative and religious universe then you have to believe in continuity and continuousness.

And if the evidence is that people have these experiences and therefore one postulates the existence of the soul, it's perfectly logical to say that the soul could live on after death?

Oh yes. The thing that seems rather sad about that is that you don't know now that the souls of the people that you loved are living on, but do they know that they lived? Do they have a memory? Does the soul have a memory? If the soul has a memory then it's an entirely different entity and far more interesting than if it doesn't have a memory. But when you look at the things that have been discovered in these comparatively early days of intense microscopic science, it's not impossible that when they've worked out what consciousness is then these questions will become susceptible to testing, and maybe the Christians will have been right all along . . .

Do you want to believe that you will meet people again after death?

That's very difficult. I can't believe it. Unfortunately. It would be great to meet up again. And that's what you miss. The conversation has been ended. But unfortunately I can't believe in that. It would be good to believe in it.

And does loss propel you towards faith?

I think loss propels you towards thought, and when you think about the condition in which we live, there are very few options that have really come out through the centuries with any clarity, that's the surprising thing. We're millions and millions and millions of unique human beings with individual fingerprints, each distinguishable from the other, even identical twins – millions and millions of us. Lots of people have had thoughts, written, discussed and philosophised, and yet what they come up with are very small numbers of ways, very few options, about the way that life is organised. That strikes me as being rather curious.

So do you expect God to come knocking on your door?

I don't think so. In fact, the idea of God being personally interested in me, you or any other individual seems to me to be, again, something that I simply can't take on board. When you're a kid you think it's *you*. It's ridiculously arrogant that you think he takes notice of me, my best friend and so on. No, I can't believe that at all. One of the greatest phrases I heard in the last two or three years was Isaac Newton's answer to someone who asked him how he discovered the laws of gravity, which changed life profoundly, and he said, 'By thinking on it continually.' And I keep thinking about that phrase and think that if I keep thinking on things continually . . . you never know what will happen.

(1995 conversation)

Paul Davies

Paul Davies is Professor of Natural Philosophy at the
University of Adelaide, and has held academic appoint-
ments at the universities of London, Cambridge and
Newcastle upon Tyne. He has achieved an international
reputation through his ability to communicate scientific
ideas to a wide audience, through print and broadcast
media. He has won many awards for his contributions to
science and philosophy.

*When you embarked on your career as a theoretical physicist, could you
ever have imagined that you'd win the Templeton Prize, the world's
most prestigious and valuable award for a contribution to thinking
about religion?*

The Templeton Prize didn't exist at that time, but I suppose the
answer is 'Yes', because I first got turned on to science by pondering
what we might call the deep questions of existence. Like all young
people, I used to lie awake at night worrying . . . 'What am I doing
here? What will happen when I die? How did the universe begin?
Will it go on for ever? Does space go on for ever? What is time?' All
these things used to bother me, and I guess they bother most young

people. But most young people grow up! I never grew up and these things still bother me. I did see my scientific work as a way of tackling these great questions of existence, even as long ago as my teens.

In your Templeton Prize address, which you called 'Physics and the Mind of God', you echoed the title of your most celebrated book, The Mind of God. *But a lot of people would see those two as almost a contradiction in terms, and they'd ask, 'What's physics to do with spirituality?'*

One way I sometimes express this is by saying that if you are a biologist and you get stuck, you might go to a chemist to help you out. If a chemist gets stuck, you might get a physicist. If you're a physicist and you get stuck, there's nowhere to go expect theology, because physics is the most basic science. It's at the base of the explanatory pyramid upon which everything else is built. It deals with the fundamental laws of nature. And that inevitably prompts us to ask questions like: 'Why those laws? Where have they come from? Why are they mathematical? What does it mean? Could they be different?' Clearly these are questions on the borderline between science and philosophy, or science and theology. They are questions which, for years, were asked only by theologians and philosophers; they weren't part of science. But scientists are now tackling those age-old questions of existence which for years lay beyond the scope of science. Now, it may be hubris to suppose we scientists are going to come up with the answers, but at least we are thinking about those things. Perhaps inevitably it will be physicists and cosmologists who tackle those sorts of issues first, because their subject matter lies closest to the ground on which the whole of the rational order of the universe is rooted.

Did you ask your parents those questions when you were very little? Did it start when you were really small?

I was a dreadful pest, always asking, 'Why this?' 'Why that?' Not only of my parents, but my poor long-suffering teachers at school. One of the problems about the education system is that it does tend to discourage young people from asking questions. That's really very bad because, particularly when it comes to these deeper issues, we don't know all the answers. There isn't a ready-made collection of answers to all possible scientific questions. Science is an evolving enterprise. Indeed, one of the joys of being a scientist is that it's not a completed project. As time goes on, we discover more and more about the world, and we ask more and more questions.

Did the answers you got as a child ever lead to God?

Only in the most simplistic sense: my parents would say, 'Well that's just the way God made it. That's it. Don't ask any further questions!' Naturally, when I was very young I regarded my parents as wiser than me. Who was I to challenge that? But when I reached my teens, I began to look very critically at the whole subject of religion as well as science. For example, I can remember reading, more or less at the same time, two very influential books. One was by the British cosmologist Fred Hoyle, called *Frontiers of Astronomy*. It was all about how we may have got our understanding of the origin and nature of the universe totally wrong. The other book was *Honest to God* by John Robinson, then the Bishop of Woolwich. That was an attempt to challenge the foundation of Christian doctrine. I thought to myself: here we have two radical thinkers, both dealing with the foundations of their different but overlapping subjects, and questioning not just the received wisdom but the very basis of their beliefs.

At the same time I was beginning to ask myself the question, 'Is there such a thing as free will?' I'd learned in my school physics class how we're all made up of atoms, and that atoms obey the laws of physics. Atoms will do what atoms have to do, oblivious of what we might think about it. So the atoms in my brain will just go about their business, irrespective of whether I want to raise my arm or open my mouth. It was a great mystery to me as to how we apparently have the freedom to do what we want to do, freedom to enact bodily movement. I can remember being greatly troubled by that, and also thinking through the consequences for morality. Should we blame somebody who commits a crime, because they're just complying with the laws of physics? I remember taking this conundrum to the curate at the local church: 'How can we have freedom of the will if bodies and brains are just physical systems that comply with the laws of physics?' He didn't have the answers. Of course, nobody really does . . .

. . . I don't belong to any formal religious organisation. But I do take seriously the dialogue between science and religion, and spend a lot of time talking to scholarly ministers of religion, and philosophers of religion, too.

Can you remember a point in your adult life when this new respect you have for religion – perhaps unusual among scientists – was inspired?

I think what happened was that I discovered the existence of what we might call serious theology. I found books in the library that were dealing with theological issues in the same manner that mathematicians deal with geometrical theorems. I thought at that stage that there is obviously more intellectual depth to this subject than I had previously believed, and that it would be worth studying, rather more carefully, the various arguments for the existence of God: the cosmological argument, the theological argument, design argument, and so on . . .

A lot of people feel that there's a hopeless conflict between the scientific view of the world and the religious view. I've often said that if you sit down with a scholarly theologian who is well versed in modern science, there's almost no conflict. Theologians these days will, of course, accept that the universe came into existence with something like a Big Bang, that life originated as a perfectly natural process, even though we don't yet know what it was. They'll accept the theory of evolution. They'll even (mostly) accept that consciousness has emerged from nature, from matter, by some natural process. It seems to me that the gulf is not, then, between scientists and professional, educated theologians. It's between theologians and, if you like, the flock – people who go to church on a Sunday and expect to simply be told a story about how the world is, without having to think through the deep issues themselves.

Many theologians I know completely reject the notion of miracles – which I've always found an abhorrent idea. It seems to me that the greatest inspiration that we can gain for something like meaning or purpose of the universe is its wonderful law-like quality: the fact that there is a deep law-like structure in the world, a hidden order in nature of a mathematical form that science can reveal. The idea of a miracle and spoiling all that I find really distasteful, on scientific as well as on theological grounds.

In your Templeton Prize address, you say, 'It is impossible to be a scientist working at the frontier without being awed by the elegance, ingenuity and harmony of the law-like order of nature. In my attempts to popularise science, I am driven by the desire to share my own sense of excitement and awe.' And you say you want to share the good news. You've written very many papers, very many books in this area. The one I want to talk about is The Mind of God, *which is a very audacious concept . . .*

All of the early scientists, such as Newton and Galileo, were religious in their own way. They saw their scientific studies as uncovering God's handiwork in nature. Science came out of the intellectual ferment in Europe in the fifteenth and sixteenth centuries, under the twin influences of, on the one hand, Greek philosophy – the notion that we could come to understand the world through reasoning, that there is a rationality in nature – and, on the other hand, the tradition which began with Judaism – the belief that we live in a created world, that the universe isn't ruled by a committee, it's not arbitrary or absurd. According to this way of thinking, the universe has been set up by a deity – a designer-being – brought into existence a finite time ago, and ordered according to a definite scheme; and furthermore, that as history unfolds, humans form part of that scheme. If you put these two strands of thinking together, as did people like Galileo and Newton, they believed that they could glimpse that grand cosmic scheme – glimpse, so to speak, the mind of God in nature. Most dramatically, they felt they could see God's hand at work in the hidden mathematical order in the universe. Consider the planets going around the sun, for example; you discover that they comply with certain mathematical formulae. Newton famously discovered that the law of gravitation gives a connection between the falling apple and the notion of the moon. So there exists a deep yet hidden order that is simply not apparent in daily life. Without the scientific method you wouldn't guess it was there; you wouldn't find it in any other way.

So the early scientists perceived this natural order and its hidden mathematical content, and they thought it derived from a creator-being. Now, what happened in the centuries that followed was that science accepted the existence of a real order in nature. You can't be a scientist if you don't believe that there is some sort of order that is at least in part comprehensible to us. So you have to make two enormous assumptions – which don't have to be right. But to be a scientist, you've got to believe they're true. First, that there is a rational order in nature. Second, that we can come to understand nature, at least in part. You wouldn't bother to become a scientist if you felt it was beyond us. What an extraordinary thing this is to believe in! There is a rational, comprehensible order in nature. Why? God has been killed off as an explanation, so this astonishing rational order is left free-floating. It doesn't have any *ground*.

The difficulty for a scientist who is an out-and-out atheist is that the essence of the scientific method is to seek reasons for why things are as they are in the world. Science asserts that the world isn't arbitrary or absurd. For example, the window breaks when the stone is thrown at it because of the forces that act. It doesn't 'just happen' without reason. You expect there to be explanations for things. And there is a long chain of reasoning from any given phenomenon, down to the basic laws of physics. So scientists expect the world to be thoroughly logical and rational at every step. But then you get down to the fundamental laws, and ask, 'Why those laws? Where did they come from?' The standard atheistic response is to suddenly do a back flip and say, 'Oh well, the laws exist reasonlessly. There's *no* reason for why they are as they are – indeed, for why they exist at all. The physical universe is ultimately arbitrary and absurd.'

Following this line of thought invites us to ground the rationality of nature in cosmic absurdity. It seems to me that that is an inconsistent position. If you really do believe that the world is ordered in a rational, intelligible way and that there's a hidden mathematical basis to it all, then that basis too has to be grounded in something. Because if you just accept the rational, intelligible, ordered universe simply as a brute fact – as a package of marvels that just happens to be – then you're led to a contradiction.

If I use the word 'God', it is not in the sense of a super-being who has existed for all eternity and, like a cosmic magician, brings the universe into being at some moment in time on a whimsical basis. When I refer to 'God', it is in the sense of the rational ground in which the whole scientific enterprise is rooted. I don't believe the universe is arbitrary or absurd. I think it has something like meaning or purpose underpinning it. Of course, one must use the words 'meaning' and 'purpose' with care, but I think there's something like a meaning or a purpose in the universe, and that we human beings are, in some small but significant way, part of that meaning or purpose.

So the God-concept is the natural order of which we are a part, a conscious part?

The God I'm referring to is not really a person or a being in the usual sense. In particular, it is something that is outside of time. That is a very significant issue, and one on which there can be a very fruitful exchange, in my opinion, between physics and philosophy. Physicists think they understand something about time. In particular, Einstein showed us that time is *part of* the physical universe. It's not a backdrop against which events happen. Indeed, time is malleable: you can change it. You can warp it in the lab. Like matter, time can be manipulated. So if we want to discuss 'the explanation' of the physical world, we have to consider something that explains space and time too; something that is more basic than space and time. We have these laws that I've been talking about. Physicists regard them as eternal: they're supposed to be there, unchanging, for all time. It follows that if we're seeking God, or whatever one might want to call it, as the rational ground in which these eternal laws are rooted, then this God must also be timeless.

The difficulty in squaring that idea with the popular notion of God is that most people want a god that they can pray to and who will fix things up, a god who will be pro-active in the world, a god who would respond to prayer . . . This is a real problem already in classical theology: how do you square the notion of God the Grand

Architect of the universe – a perfect and therefore unchanging being – with a god who is involved in day-to-day human affairs and working occasional miracles? I think the latter sort of god can't be reconciled with science (though I have scientific colleagues who disagree). So when I think of God, it is as an abstract, timeless being . . . That's not much comfort to you if you want to pray to somebody for help or guidance, like making sure you're going to pass your exam the following day.

You do acknowledge and, indeed, express wonder at the patterns, the laws of the universe . . .

And so do almost all of my physics colleagues, and scientists from other disciplines, even if they would cast themselves as militant atheists. They are deeply inspired by the wonder, the beauty, the ingenuity of nature, and the underlying, law-like mathematical order. They share this inspiration.

. . . But you still reject the teleological argument – God as the designer, like some interior decorator or something. But would you say that God is design – not the designer, but Design itself? Does that approach it?

In some ways it does, because I sometimes say that it is 'as if' the universe has been designed. I don't think that there is a super-being with a project, who has figured out what the end goal ought to be and has set the universe up in order to work through that agenda. But it is certainly true when we look at nature – the way that different aspects of nature interweave with each other so felicitously and so consistently and so beautifully – that there is a conspicuous *scheme* of things. The universe is not just a hotch-potch of odds and ends thrown together in juxtaposition. One arrives at this conclusion particularly through studying the basic laws of physics and the way, for example, the laws of quantum physics, thermodynamics and gravitation interleave each other in a manner that bestows a beautiful harmony and self-consistency. It is 'as if' there is a designer . . .

Is that beyond the rational?

... It could be that there are some things that are simply going to be forever beyond scientific enquiry – not because we're lacking the money or the expertise or something of that sort, but because there are inherent limits to how far rational enquiry can take us. We know from the foundations of logic and mathematics that there are ultimate limits on things, on what can be proved and what can be known. It could be that the scientific project is limited and that there will inevitably be mystery. I think, in fact, that that is the case, that there will inevitably be *some* element of mystery in following the scientific path.

But then the question is, can we ever bridge that final gap? If science leaves us with mystery, is there a way that we can come to know about the world, about existence, not through scientific enquiry but through some other method? I'm open-minded as to whether that is the case. I'm talking here about revelatory or mystical experiences, where somehow the answer is grasped – not through rational enquiry, not through experimentation, but by 'knowing' in some internal sense. I've never had a mystical or revelatory experience. Maybe I will one day...

So you see the universe as mysterious, but in your own words, 'a coherent, rational, elegant and harmonious expression of a deep and powerful meaning' – which is very poetic. How should the person who might be adrift, full of doubt, and longing for a kind of belief – how should he or she interpret that meaning that you sing with such admiration?

By believing that we *do* have a place. We've emerged from nature. We *belong* here in the universe as part of the natural order. To be sure, we're not at the centre of the universe; we're not the pinnacle of creation or anything of that sort. But nevertheless we do have a place. I think that the existence of not just conscious minds, but of beings who can also make *sense* of the world, is a fact of staggering importance. I don't know if that provides inspiration to people. But I hope they will feel that human beings are at least special in that sense...

You call us 'animated stardust . . .'

Not only animated stardust. We're stardust capable of understanding how the stars came to exist in the first place.

You say none of this is going to help somebody praying that God will help them pass their exams – and that's a trivial example. But what about the problem of pain and of suffering and of grief, and what happens when we die, and those big questions, which I'm sure you thought about in the darkness of the night when you were young? Have you had experiences in your own life when the intellectual passion for the ideas that you are describing wasn't enough?

Yes. Because, of course, nothing I have said deals with the sort of issues we struggle with in daily life, which are ethical and moral issues. The weakness of restricting to a God who's just some sort of abstract, mathematical, rational ground for the world is that it doesn't provide us with any sort of moral guidance. Most people turn to religion not because they want to understand how the universe is put together, but because they want to understand how their own lives are put together, and what they should do next. You don't go to a physicist to ask about right and wrong . . . But I also have these struggles and concerns.

What about issues like life after death? Do you believe that, as animated stardust, we just go back into the universe?

I normally answer that in a very evasive way by saying, 'We don't understand consciousness, so how can we say anything about the cessation of consciousness?' In other words, if we don't know what it is in the brain that gives rise to consciousness, how can we talk about its survival when there is no brain? But that really is a fudge. Of course, it's possible to be religious and not believe in life after death, and it's possible to believe in life after death and not be religious. They really are disconnected things. It's very hard for a physicist to believe consciousness is going to survive death. On the other hand, stranger things have happened, and I suppose I'm open-minded about it. However, I'm not too sure what this post-death state is going to be. Do I have a body, and where's that going to come from? Do I have memories of my life? If I don't, then in what sense is it me? What am I going to be doing with myself, subsequent to death? Am I going to be in some realm where very little happens for all eternity? That's not terribly appealing. So mostly I find that what is on offer, in terms of life after death, is really rather unpalatable.

The older I get, the more I find that I am returning to those deep questions, and asking 'Why?' I don't think it's enough to shrug this question aside. My scientific colleagues will often say, 'Scientists shouldn't ask "why?" questions.' Well, that response reminds me of my school days: 'Sit down, Davies, and shut up!' I'm afraid I'm not going to sit down, and I'm not going to shut up. I'm going to go on asking these 'why?' questions. We do want to know *why* the world is as it is. Why did it come to exist 13.7 billion years ago in a Big Bang? Why are the laws of electromagnetism and gravitation as they are? Why *those* laws? What are *we* doing here? And, in particular, how come we are able to *understand* the world? Why is it that we're equipped with intellects that can unpick all this wonderful cosmic order and make sense of it? It's truly astonishing.

(2002 conversation)

Christopher Frayling

Professor Sir Christopher Frayling has been Rector and Vice-Provost of the Royal College of Arts since 1996, as well as Professor of Cultural History. An historian and prolific critic, broadcaster and journalist, he has served on innumerable arts committees and published many books on subjects as various as Jean Jacques Rousseau and the spaghetti Western.

'Devout sceptics' . . . It means you're serious about questioning, serious about the quest, serious about seeking answers, but you're not quite satisfied with the answers that you're getting. I think it's a sort of serious-mindedness. 'Devout' equals 'serious-minded'. One isn't flippant about it. One doesn't cast aside these big questions because they're naff or out of fashion. One takes them seriously . . . So it's always getting beyond the surface appearances of everyday life, and the surface explanations of everyday life, into something a little bit more.

I think it began when I was at school, really. I was at a public school. Went away to boarding school when I was six – which I think is a trifle early. Aged twelve to seventeen, late 1950s, early 1960s – nearer *Tom Brown's Schooldays* than a modern establishment in some ways. Chapel once a day, on pain of punishment, and sometimes twice. And I was thinking, 'Hang on. They're chucking all this stuff at me that's supposed to be about religion and spirituality. It's got *nothing* whatsoever to do with something I can identify with.' And I think that disjunction is where I started, between the inner person and the external traffic.

. . . One of the nice things about teenage years, I think, is that you're not frightened to grapple with the huge questions which, in your twenties, you suddenly stop grappling with. You have to get on with everyday life. Things get smaller. But it's great to ask cosmic questions when you're about fifteen, isn't it? The meaning of life, and all that.

Did you come from a family which was religious?

My mother was a free thinker to the extent that she didn't want me baptised because she said I should make up my own mind. And, in fact, I was baptised when I was fifteen . . . My father, who came from a military background, had a kind of 'church parade' attitude to religion. He went every Sunday, he loved the hymns. He used to cry at the first line of 'Abide with Me' – it got him going. And occasionally we'd go to the Guards' Chapel in Birdcage Walk. I went with him once, and absolutely loved walking through: these people would jump to attention as he walked by, as he went into chapel; all these banners, tattered remnants of battles of the past . . .

Did you share your father's emotions at the great hymns?

I still do, actually. It's very comforting. I've only got to hear certain hymns. There's one that we used to sing every night at Evensong at school: 'God be in my head and in my understanding, God be at my end and at my departing, God be in my eyes, and in my seeing . . .' all this. I've only got to hear that: the eyes start prickling, even now. There's certain carols . . . It's a wonderful, warm cocoon. But I sang them once a day for over ten years, so they're part of my culture, they're in my head. The phrases come out when I'm grasping for a cliché, when I'm writing – it's always a hymn. It's there. It's a repertoire.

And do you respond to the liturgy, as well as the hymns? 'Lamb of God, who taketh away the sins of the world . . .' Does that do it for you as well?

Not so much. The thing that stuck in my craw, even then – although I may be post-rationalising – was phrases like 'whose service is perfect freedom', 'the love that asks no question' and things like that, because I've always had a sort of questioning attitude to life. I like to unpick things. I like to take them to pieces, find out how they work. I was really quite rebellious about 'whose service is perfect freedom'. I don't like that thought, that serving somebody completely is a kind of freedom . . .

When I was at university, in the mid 1960s, the great breakthrough for me, where the actual content of religion was concerned, was reading Jean Jacques Rousseau, the eighteenth-century Genevan philosopher – a book called *Emile,* which is all about education. There's a water-tight subsection of this book which is an open letter to the Archbishop of Paris by Rousseau: a brilliant rejection of institutional religion, of intermediaries between the individual and their spirituality, or their god – and all the kind of empirical aspects of religion. It's a rejection of all that, in favour of a personalised, 'listening to your inner voice', conscience kind of religion. And it had a huge impact on me.

Rousseau subsequently wrote a wonderful book that's very neglected, called *The Dreams of a Solitary Walker* – the last thing he wrote. It's all about going for a long walk and thinking those kinds of thoughts as you're surrounded by nature or whatever it is. It's not God through nature, and it's not a kind of privatised religion, which I don't like at all – you know, the modern, New-Agey kind of privatised version. It's just a quiet conversation with a kind of personal god, although he doesn't call it God – it's a supreme being. God, he thinks, is too gendered: a chap with a beard from the Old Testament.

This had a huge impact because I was trying to find someone who'd written about the sort of journey that was analogous in a way to mine – finding all these external trappings rather constraining. And I found it in Rousseau. He really knocked me sideways. Remember also that this is 1968, Paris, all roads lead to student rebellion, so Rousseau was *it*. Rousseau was the sort of Che Guevara of Paris at that time.

So did you associate Rousseau with a generalised rebellion, a great quest for freedom which was not in service, but in questioning?

Yes, exactly. I was at Cambridge for six years – undergraduate and then PhD. I was surrounded by astro-physicians, biologists, physicists, who thought they were squeezing God, or any need for God, out of explanations of how things tick. And so I associated Rousseau with the thought that actually there were some jolly big questions that they weren't asking. The 'why?' questions, rather than the 'how?' questions. Even today, when I hear Richard Dawkins talking about it – and he's very extreme – it upsets me. The arrogance. It's bad science, bad philosophy, to be so shrill: 'We don't need God. We don't need cheap supernatural explanations,' as he once put it.

In the late 1960s, too, I remember people were saying the same thing. I kept saying, 'Yes, but actually you can analyse the Big Bangs, you can look at the origin of the universe, you can look at evolution, but all it does is put the question about God into a deeper place than it was before, i.e. why have all the elements ended up in the way that they have?' That's not a question that scientists ask. So I found Rousseau a way of challenging the arrogance, I thought, of those sort of questions. He's a 'why?' person, not a 'how?' person.

Historically, men and women created religion roughly at the same time that they created art – and both were attempts to find meaning.

That's exactly right – the question of art. Because I went through a very similar journey where art was concerned. At school, like everybody else in the late 1950s, one associated religion with Holman Hunt, *The Light of the World* – this extraordinary painting done in the 1850s. Incredibly meticulous detail: the most empirical painting of a deity that's ever been done. Every leaf is very well studied . . . Facts, facts, facts. Gentle Jesus, meek and mild, knocking at the door. When I was at school, prints and reproductions in every prayer book – that was the image.

And again, it was at university that I discovered a very important piece of writing by a Russian painter, Kandinsky, called *On the Spiritual in Art,* published in 1911, which is a formidable piece of writing. He reminisces about going to an exhibition in Germany where he sees people looking at a landscape, looking at a floral painting, looking at a sunset, looking at a sunrise, looking at lots and lots of crucifixions. They consulted their catalogues – who painted it? when was it painted? – and the connoisseurs were all talking about technique. And he says, 'But nothing's happening in this exhibition. Hungry souls go hungry away.' And the people who might ask interesting questions about the paintings aren't asking them. What about a kind of painting where the spirituality comes from inside? So he started a journey towards abstraction, from figurative work, as part of this journey of trying to express the spirituality on canvas, getting away from those facts, those pieces of information – *The Light of the World* philosophy – into something that's much more to do with the inner person. And I read that when I was twenty-one, and it's really stayed with me. I'm not saying all painters are on this quest. Only some painters are interested in those sort of questions.

I simultaneously saw the paintings of Mark Rothko, 1950s New York paintings, where he was doing precisely that: a sort of quest for spiritual calm through colour, through abstraction, through just the organisation of the elements – not through imagery, not through literal things. He was saying, 'If there is a God, I don't want a God that I can understand. I want something bigger than that.' And the way to approach that is through abstraction. It's not through reducing it all the time to facts. I think Rothko's paintings still are the most moving paintings I've ever, ever encountered. It's like when you close your eyes and the colours you get when you're not looking at the world. That's what his paintings are like, and it's so poignant because he felt that he was in the wilderness, that he was going through a sort of dark night of the soul, trying to make sense of it all in this way, through this abstraction, and I think he got to where Kandinsky was trying to get in 1911 . . .

You could see God in Rothko?

Absolutely. And also *a* god. It wasn't a specific god, it wasn't even necessarily a Christian god. It was a *something* beyond the facts of everyday life. You've got to explain why, about 70,000 years ago, suddenly, in south-west Europe, Lascaux and Altamira and all these other caves, and simultaneously in Africa, people started doing art depicting bison and antelopes and all sorts of horned creatures on the walls of caves. What are they doing? They want to express something. There's something more than the facts of feeding yourself, sexual reproduction, and so on. There's more. And no one knows why. Is it to do with magic? Is it to do with taming those creatures by representing them on the wall? What was the impulse? I don't know, but it happens, and it happens at a certain stage in evolution. And no evolutionary biologist can explain that kind of consciousness. It sort of happens, and it's a very important part of life . . .

Do you go to church?

Periodically. My wife, Helen, is a Roman Catholic. We have a house in the west of Ireland, where the entire community revolves around Sunday Mass, and I go every Sunday to church when we're in the west of Ireland. In the rest of the year, I go about once a month – not regularly and not to the same church. The other thing is, you see, I love architecture. I love the physical environment of churches, and I don't want to suggest that I'm a sort of religious tourist, but that helps me.

I did a TV programme all about the building of Chartres Cathedral in 1994, and it was just so wonderful to be able to get into that building, get into the fabric of it. We spent a week in the building, removed all the seats, removed all the post-mediaeval traces – an empty building as it would have been in 1194–1220 or whenever it was when it was built – and being able to clamber round the roof and get to all these sorts of places. It was just miraculous. And the best thing about Chartres, from the point of view of our conversation, is that on the Royal Portal, the great entrance, you've got all these scientists: geometry, arithmetic, mathematics, algebra; and the Greeks are all there. And above them Mary, the mother of God, sort of presiding over science. I like that. Corbusier might have called it a machine for meditating in.

You said that you weren't drawn to the sort of New Age-type philosophy, which is fairly pick 'n' mix, isn't it? But in a sense, what you're describing is also pick 'n' mix.

In a way. What I don't like is the self-actualisation stuff, the idea of the sort of development of the self, rather like going to the gym for physical jerks; you do all this self-actualisation stuff to tune yourself up spiritually. I don't like that. I really don't. I think religion must have something to do with community, with working together, with creativity, with asking – things that can be shared.

All your career, you've been involved with design in many ways, and the Royal College of Art has a famous design department. When you look at the universe, do you see a grand design?

That's very interesting, because the word 'design' only came to mean what it means today – i.e. the making of products, industrial design, graphic design, car design – in the mid-nineteenth century. If you asked someone in the sixteenth, seventeenth, eighteenth century what the word 'design' meant, they'd say, 'It means God.' It does precisely mean the reality behind appearances, the fact that it all ultimately makes sense in some way: the grand design. I do sort of believe that. But it's designed without a designer, in a sense. I don't like the Old Testament idea of this chap with a long beard who gets terribly angry all the time, sort of designing things all the time, putting the chess pieces in – a puppet master. I don't like that idea. An important aspect of all this for me is free will, is God standing back, is possibly putting the elements there which come together in this particular universe. But then, the crucial thing is standing back and letting us do what we want with it. Because otherwise – I think it's known as the 'theodity problem' – the problem is how do you explain evil? How do you explain the *Titanic* in a world that's supposed to be run by a benevolent god? That's an insoluble problem unless you believe in free will. We're allowed to let rip, and if we want to make a mess of it, we make a mess of it. It's in our hands. God's at one remove from all that.

So it's design. The elements were there – the Big Bang happened out of something, it didn't happen out of nothing – and a particular combination of elements led to where we are now, the state of human consciousness, which is an incredible journey. But not every step of the way was designed. It's not an interventionist god, the god of the gaps, the god that explains things we can't understand. It's not that sort of god. It's much more removed from everyday reality than that. So, yes, it is a grand design, but the design is very much in our hands, out of elements that we didn't necessarily invent.

You've described a personal journey asking questions – not so much finding answers to them, but asking them. Are you content with where you are in this process?

No, never. Got to keep moving. In everything, you've got to keep developing. You've got to leave yourself open to questions. One good example of this: Adam and Eve in the Garden of Eden. I always think the Garden of Eden sounds incredibly boring, where everything's sorted out; there's answers to all the questions, and everything's hunky dory. When Eve gives the apple to Adam and he eats of the fruit of the tree of knowledge, suddenly life becomes interesting. You enter real life; you ask questions; you're a sceptical, questioning, conscious human being. That's so much more interesting than Paradise. Paradise sounds pretty boring to me – you know, where everything's sorted out, everything's solved. You step into this world of complexity and creativity and interest, and that's a much more fun place to be, in my opinion. I'm with the fruit!

(2002 conversation)

Denis Healey

Baron Healey of Riddlesden is judged to be one of the most significant British political figures of the post-war period. Born in 1917, he distinguished himself during the Second World War, and entered Parliament as a Labour MP in 1952. He held high office – Secretary of State for Defence, Chancellor of the Exchequer and Deputy Leader of the Labour Party – has published sixteen books, and has always shown a passionate interest in the arts.

I began to think about what you might broadly call 'matters of the spirit' when I was probably twelve or thirteen, and was constructing theories of the universe and trying to answer unanswerable questions like 'Does everything have a cause? And in that case, did the world ever begin or was it from everlasting?' Those things interested me a great deal. Also, when I was a boy in Keighley, we looked over the town to Haworth where the Brontë sisters lived and they influenced me a great deal, particularly Emily, who I think was not religious in the conventional sense. As far as I know she wasn't much of a churchgoer, although her father was a parson. But she wrote some of the greatest mystical verse ever, I think, which I often quote.

Can you explain what you mean by mysticism?

Well, as a sense of 'something far more deeply interfused', to quote Wordsworth: that there is a reality beyond what we see and touch and smell. This is a thing which has always – and increasingly, I think – intrigued me. I did philosophy when I was a student at Oxford, and was enormously influenced by Kant who, in his own words, 'destroyed reason to make room for belief'. I think he showed conclusively that you can't apply the sort of reasoning which produces the microwave oven or the atomic bomb to questions of value, and therefore, in a sense, ruled out theology. But he did it in order to make people believe in things which can't be proved by scientific logic. Pascal, who was a great religious philosopher and did believe in the Christian God, always insisted that opposite things can be true at the same time; and I was led by the Master of Balliol away from the conventional philosophers to people like Kierkegaard, who was a very tortured Protestant Christian . . .

I have a picture of you as a boy, a young man, wanting to find explanations for things, which is a very rational approach, and yet looking out and thinking of Emily Brontë and that which is mystical, spiritual. Was there a tension between these two sides?

I wouldn't say there was because, again, I was led to Greek philosophers like Heraclitus, who say, 'Everything is in flux. Nothing is ever the same. It changes all the time,' and the early Christian philosopher Tertullian, who said, 'I believe it because it's incredible. It's certain because it's impossible.' To understand the most important things, you have to accept that they are what Blake called 'contraries', which are not negatives. There are things which coexist at the same time.

There's one particular passage of Blake I like very much which expresses this view. He said, 'All Bibles or sacred codes have been the causes of the following errors: that Man has two real existing principles: there's a body and a soul; that energy, called Evil, is alone from the body, and that reason, called Good, is alone from the soul.' And he finishes up: 'But the following contraries to these are true. Man has no body distinct from his soul, for that called "body" is a portion of the soul discerned by the five senses, the chief inlets of soul in this age. Energy is the only life, and it's from the body. And reason is the bound, or outward circumference, of energy. Energy is eternal delight.' That's my motto!

You've written, 'I've never been able to accept the theology and dogma of the Church. I preferred the ethical Christianity of Tolstoy's later years.' Can you explain what you mean by ethical Christianity?

Well, Tolstoy believed in God and, indeed, wrote a lot of short stories of a religious nature which were intended to instruct the peasantry among whom he worked. And of course, he was tremendously obsessed by death. One of his greater short stories was called *The Death of Ivan Ilyitch,* and it's how a wealthy peasant, towards the end of his life, suddenly realises that his life is going to end and begins to wonder what all that really means. But essentially, I think he believed that all men are brothers – and that I believe, too – but you can believe that without believing literally that there is a heavenly Father and that we're all his children.

Partly, I think, because of reading the great philosophers, I've been very reluctant to accept any sort of theology. I think the moment you start freezing feelings about the spirit into propositions which have a systematic relationship with one another, like oppositions in chemistry or physics, you cripple and deform the real spirit. And even worse, of course, is when you then get institutions called churches built to represent one particular theology rather than another – which have been responsible, I would think, for half the wars in history, and indeed are responsible for half the wars going on at the present time.

And yet, wouldn't it be true to say at the same time that you believe in a brotherhood of man, which is the humanistic belief? You were a communist when you were a young man and then you were a socialist. Isn't that also codifying a faith in the perfectibility of mankind?

No. I don't believe that mankind is perfectible, but you can aim to be better. History is not a steady progress from the depths to the heights. It's an uncertain process, although we have a duty to make things better. I think the idea, for example, that politicians can make all men happy is ridiculous. Happiness comes not from government or anything like that. It comes from something inside people. But I think the politician does have a duty to remove unnecessary obstacles to happiness.

You've had very good friends and colleagues throughout your life who have been practising Christians. Did you ever feel that they had something you didn't have?

I haven't actually felt impoverished by it. The nearest thing I've had to a major mystical experience in recent times was on my first ever visit to India with Edna, where I visited the observatory set up by an eighteenth-century rajah in Jaipaur who was a Hindu but got all the latest books from Newton and so on. And wandering in this extraordinary wilderness of cubes and triangles . . . the observatory is entirely built out of enormous monolithic blocks of one sort or another. I think the tension I felt then brought to mind lines from my favourite writer, Yeats:

> A moonlit or a starlit dome disdains
> All that Man is, those mere complexities
> The fury and the mire of human veins.

Now that is a wonderful description of the Muslim approach to architecture and religion . . .

It seems as if you are drawn towards what I will call 'God' – as a shorthand – by beauty.

I think there are two main routes into the spiritual world for ordinary people. Outside churches is nature, which has often inspired people with mystical feelings. You remember Emily Brontë talking about the Yorkshire Moors:

> What have those lonely mountains worth revealing?
> More glory and more grief than I can tell.
> The earth that wakes one human heart to feeling
> Can centre both the worlds of Heaven and of Hell.

And Wordsworth, of course – his spiritual experiences are very, very much connected with nature, and sometimes he got very fed up with the Christian Church because he felt it was too confining.

The other great route, of course, is through the arts. I find some of the music of Bach and Beethoven – particularly his last quartets – and of Mozart, leads you to these realities more directly than anything else, but so does a great deal of painting, particularly, perhaps, Mantegna and Piero della Francesca in Italian painting.

You've written that you feel it's impossible fully to experience Bach, Beethoven, Mantegna, Dostoevsky, without an appreciation of the spiritual dimension.

Well, they are about the spirit, and if you're blind to that you won't fully appreciate them.

You could deconstruct them if you were a modernist, I suppose.

Well, if you would rather pick your own nose and examine the snot than smell the perfume of eternity, that's all right. I don't mind. But what an impoverishment of the human spirit that type of post-modernism is . . .

We talk of spirit and soul. Are they the same for you?

When I use them, they are the same. But of course, many people use them differently. A lot of people use the word 'soul' to mean the individual human soul which survives the body and, according to the body's behaviour in life, goes either to heaven or hell or limbo, purgatory, somewhere in between.

I do believe that we all have souls, but I am not at all sure about the eternal life of the soul, and still less of the reincarnation of the soul. The Hindus believe in it, or some of the Hindu sects . . .

You talk about the limitations of knowledge, and indeed, of language. Are there not points, when one is thinking or talking of the spirit, when the only appropriate thing is silence?

Silence or music. Exactly. Great modern philosophers like Wittgenstein spent their lives pointing this out and then decided philosophy was a waste of time: you'd better do something more useful because you couldn't use words and propositions and sentences to explore these problems beyond that point . . .

What sort of life after death can you conceive of?

If there is a life after death, of course it will be a life of the soul. There's no doubt about that. But whether it does survive death, I'm not convinced. But again, if I can quote my dear old friend Yeats, when he wrote about the way people change throughout life:

And now his Wars with God begin
At the stroke of Midnight, God shall win.

Like most of us, you've experienced bereavement. At times like that, did you want to believe you would see those loved ones again?

I wouldn't say that really, no. I always remember, when my father died – he was ninety-two and he was cremated – when we went to bury the ashes in the cemetery somewhere in east London, I always remember the clergyman saying to my mother something like 'Don't worry, you'll be meeting him again soon.' And that seemed to me slightly shocking. And Mother didn't really believe it, although when we got back to her house, it was the first time I ever remember in my life seeing her crying. I cry like a fish all the time, but Mother cried very, very rarely.

When my mother died, at the age of ninety-nine, I was conscious of my own loss. I'd sat with her when she died in a nursing home, during the last few hours. She became totally unconscious and her breath rattled. She had lost so much of herself in the last few years – only the last few years. She was extremely vital intellectually in responding to things like flowers and the children until she was about ninety-six. But the last two or three years there was a very rapid deterioration, and I didn't feel a great sense of loss then. In some ways I felt more when one of my best friends died. He was American. He'd broken his back in a minor motor accident, and had had a very difficult period for the last fifteen years of his life. And I felt that more because he was very much younger. But suddenly the effort of getting himself strapped up in metal frameworks so that he could move just became too much for him. And I felt the tragedy of that in some sense more, because it was unnaturally early. Some of my friends who've been religious have lost their religion when they've been hit by a blow like that. They feel God cannot be all-powerful and all-good if he lets this happen. I have never been tormented by that because I've never believed in an all-powerful personal god.

If somebody who you loved very much – one of your family – was very, very ill, would you pray? Have you prayed?

No, I don't think I would, because there'd be nobody to pray to. For me.

So do you call yourself an atheist?

Oh no, I wouldn't call myself an atheist or an agnostic. I believe that there is a life of the spirit which, to me, is in the end much more important than the rest of my life, my political life or whatever. But I don't believe in a personal god to whom I would pray and who could respond. Do you see what I mean? And indeed, very few religions believe in a personal god in that sense, to whom you can pray and ask him to do you a kindness or a service. The interesting thing about the Christian religion is that it is very much centred in a way on everyday life – works are as important as faith. You can ask God to help you in good works. I think even more so, really, in Judaism. But I think that many Christians, on the other hand, have said, 'Religion is what a man is when he is alone.' And oddly enough, when I took my scholarship exam for Balliol, that was the general knowledge question we had to answer in our essay: is that true or not?

Do you think it's true?

No, I don't think it is, because I think, again, we are not alone, anyway, are we? We are all linked with one another, spiritually as well as in all sorts of social and political and economic nexuses.

This takes us back to your youth and that passionate belief in the brotherhood of man, the ethical Christianity you found so attractive. Have you not been disappointed by the proofs that come in daily that in fact man fails?

I'm appalled when I pick up the papers. But then I was taught by people like Kierkegaard not to expect a perfect world.

Are you ever tempted to withdraw more and more into the world that you've described that matters so much to you, which is the world of art, music . . . ?

I've always believed in living in more than one world, like Traherne. This is another thing: I don't want to cop out of the sufferings of real people living at this time by pursuing my private interests, but I hope that the pursuit of my private interests may help me a little bit in understanding some of these other problems.

As one gets old, inevitably one thinks of one's own death. Is this something which you contemplate?

I don't worry about it. I mean, I know I shall die sometime. I think with the wonders of modern science and having chosen my parents very carefully – as I say, they lived to ninety-two and ninety-nine – I may have a fair time ahead before my faculties make life not worth living. But I don't agonise over it the way that Ivan Ilyitch did in Tolstoy's novel.

You quoted Yeats, the poem which ends 'At the stroke of midnight, God shall win'... Do you think that's true?

I don't know. People always ask me, 'Are you enjoying the House of Lords?' And I say, 'Well, it's not a verb you would use about the House of Lords, but it's comfortable, and clubbable.' And so they say, 'Are you enjoying life?' I say, 'Yes. I believe it's a great deal better than the alternative.' And then I say, 'But I'm not sure.'

(1995 conversation)

John Humphrys

One of the best-known broadcasters of his generation, John Humphrys has presented the *Today* programme on BBC Radio 4 since 1987, and he is famous (and feared) for his penetrating, no-nonsense style of interviewing. He has written two books, *Devil's Advocate* and *The Great Food Gamble*, and has an abiding interest in the cause of organic farming.

What sort of things make you wonder?

Well, all the entirely obvious and clichéd things that you'd expect: hunger and disease, and generosity, kindness, beauty – all sorts of things. Absolutely everything makes you wonder, and I suppose it's the obvious question, isn't it: why beauty lives alongside ugliness, and why generosity lives alongside meanness of spirit, and why wealth lives alongside poverty and obesity lives alongside famine. Why on earth, in a country like this or the United States, do we spend huge fortunes trying to get slim while people in most countries in the world would love a tiny tiny bit of that money to be able to eat properly, for instance?

Have you always asked those questions?

Yes, I think so. Well, as long as I've been able to think about it. I can't ever remember not asking those questions. I can remember standing on a disused World War II airfield in Pengham in Cardiff – and the thing about old airfields is the space around you – and it was a perfect night with lots of stars. I was very young and we'd been out fooling around, as kids. I suppose I was seven or eight, and it was the usual thing – you look at the sky and it's huge and you start to wonder, 'What's outside it all?' Oh, God! And that's the sort of first problem you have, isn't it, really? After the questions about death. I remember coming back on a bus from Aberystwyth and I suddenly realised that I was going to die and it shattered me completely, absolutely shattered me. Again, I suppose I was six or seven, and I thought, 'What's the point of being here, then, if that's how it's going to end?' Nobody said anything – it just happened. And I thought, 'Well, that's it, then. Barmy, isn't it? The whole thing is just rather silly.'

Did you have a personal view about God? Did you imagine him to be a man with a beard, or wasn't he real to you?

It didn't occur to me because I'd been going to church all my life, I mean, obviously I was baptised and later on I was confirmed. It didn't occur to me that God did not exist. I took that for granted. It was just the sort of thing that you were fed with your mother's milk. It was many years before I questioned it at all, and I went through a period in my very early teens of being quite religious. For some reason, and I can't imagine now why, I decided that I had to read the Bible through from cover to cover – a pretty boring thing for a thirteen-year-old to do. Can you imagine: 'So-and-so begat so-and-so who begat . . . ?' I went through the whole bit. I kept a little notebook and each day filled in the last bit I'd read so that I didn't miss anything out. I did it without any fervour. There was no kind of evangelical thing; this was just a chore that I'd set myself for reasons that I now can't understand. It bored me rigid. I got absolutely no spiritual sustenance from it or anything of the sort . . .

So the outcome was what? You didn't feel closer to God, but did it make you feel that perhaps the whole thing was a waste of time?

No. I didn't feel closer to God, that's absolutely true. I think I was never close to God. I did it because I thought you had to do it. Because I thought everybody did it and I kept, I suppose, looking for signs, looking for proof of God's existence. Still am, I suppose . . . We do this for the rest of our lives, and some find it and others don't. I didn't, really.

Did this coincide with the development of a trait which I know you've said you have, which is that of questioning authority? It would be natural to question authority in the Church, and God second?

Yes. I'm not sure which came first, but yes, that's absolutely right, there is a coincidence there. Certainly I've always questioned authority. The vicar was a hugely authoritarian figure. You didn't mess with the vicar, especially the High Church, although it was in Wales – not the Church *of* Wales, as in the Church of England, but the Church *in* Wales. I couldn't quite work out as a tiny tot what made him different. I couldn't see that he was in any way different from my father or anybody else. I couldn't quite see what the point of the vicar was, I suppose, and I couldn't really quite see what the point of the Church was. I'm not sure that I can still . . .

Do you think there was a period when you were eleven or twelve when, thinking back on the fact that your mother – your whole family – had suffered this terrible bereavement with the loss of your baby sister Christine, you felt angry with God?

I felt angry. I certainly felt angry quite early on. I blamed the death of Christine as much as anything, I think, on the fact that we were poor. Christine died of gastro-enteritis and she shouldn't have, I think. Certainly my father thought that at the time. Had she had better medical care then it wouldn't have happened, we think. Now that may or may not be true, but nonetheless that was what we believed – that we didn't have the right sort of treatment and she died of a disease from which babies should not die. At the time, I kind of associated the Church a bit with all of that. I couldn't quite see why the vicar should live in what seemed to me at the time a terribly grand house and do rather well out of it. All pretty childish stuff, I know, but there you are, that's how I was as a child. And I suppose I did think – and obviously I've thought since about it – what's the point? Why does God put a little tot on earth and then see her off after a very short time? It causes grief to such a lot of people. I've never worked that out, and I've never found the answers of the various vicars and bishops and archbishops that I've spoken to since very satisfactory. So yes, it all comes together, I suppose.

But it's one thing to ask that question and another to accept the fact that there are no answers.

It's got to be faith we're talking about . . . I'm sorry. I didn't ever say, 'I do not believe in God,' because I'm not that certain. I really am the most appalling, wishy-washy agnostic you will ever meet in a long life. I find it terribly difficult . . . but if there is absolutely nothing, no guiding force, no moral guiding force, or immoral guiding force for that matter, what is conscience? Why do we alone of the species have this thing called conscience, and why do some of us make a reasonable living out of beating old ladies over the head and nicking their handbags and some of us don't? . . . So I'm not sure that I don't believe. If there were no God – I wish there were another word to use, but anyway for the purposes of this conversation it's good enough – then why do we have a conscience? It's not just for the survival of the species, is it? Loads of species survive and they do dreadful things to each other all the time, not just occasionally. We do dreadful things occasionally, of course, like the Holocaust and so on, but other species survive and make a habit of eating each other routinely.

Do you believe in the existence of evil?

Yes, yes I do. It's manifest, isn't it? You can't not believe in the existence of evil. Fred West was evil. Adolph Hitler was evil. There's no question about it.

And so the other polarity as well . . . ?

Precisely. That's the other bit of the problem. Well, perhaps what we're talking about is the existence of good, not the existence of God, and again, manifestly, you must believe in the existence of good because you see good people . . .

Do you have any sympathy with the famous thought that was uttered by Enoch Powell when he said that he didn't like listening to music because it awakened thoughts that couldn't be fulfilled?

Yes, I do, because the best music lifts you to a peak, doesn't it? You can't stay there – it's a brief moment. But that's the point, that's what life's about. Those brief moments. The bits that you remember. The bits that lifted you lasted, usually, for very short periods of time. The moment you saw your child's face for the first time will stay with you all your life, won't it? The moment you first heard and began to get a sense of what it was all about in a Beethoven quartet will stay with you for ever. The moment you read a book that moved you to tears will stay with you for ever . . .

Do you believe in the soul?

Does it survive after the body, do you mean? An out-of-body thing? I don't know. Again, it goes back to the problem that I have all along with this: is there something that continues after you're reduced to ashes or the worms have eaten you? I don't know. I want to but I can see no reason to believe it. To get beyond the physical into the metaphysical, I find terribly difficult. To get beyond the physical into anything.

But you'd like to?

Of course. That's the ultimate experience, isn't it? Maybe what you're experiencing when you hear a piece of wonderful music or read a book that moves you or see a child's face – a child free of guilt and untainted by the impurities of life. They move you, of course, and you feel sometimes, for the odd brief moment, that you've grasped something, and then it's gone. I suppose the people to be envied are the ones who manage to hold on to those things for longer, maybe, and to even summon them at will, which is I suppose what real faith, real belief, real spirituality is about, isn't it? There are those, no doubt, who experience none of that, and they are perhaps the truly amoral people. They're certainly people to be pitied. But there are those at the far end of the scale who seem able to live in a kind of spiritual treasure-house. They seem able to find these things for themselves and hold on to them. I don't know how they do that.

You sound wistful when you describe those people.

Oh yes. Aren't we all? What's happiness? Each of us has our own moments of happiness and definitions of happiness, but ultimately the good meal, the walk on the cliff tops, the concert that lifts your spirits briefly – they are fleeting, aren't they? That's the whole point, and maybe all life is is a collection of those sometimes sublime moments and the rest is a life of quiet desperation. But it would be rather nice if you could kind of turn that around a bit, wouldn't it? Rather less of the quiet desperation and rather more of the sublime moments. Golly – that would be all right. I 'wist' for that.

(1997 conversation)

James Lovelock

James Lovelock is an independent scientist, environmentalist, author and Doctor *Honoris Causa* of several universities throughout the world. As the author of *The Gaia Theory* and *The Ages of Gaia*, which consider the planet earth as a self-regulated living being, he is considered one of the main ideological leaders in the history of the development of environmental awareness. Recently he published an autobiography, *Homage to Gaia*.

You've described yourself as an agnostic. Can you start by explaining what you mean by that?

I suppose it originally means 'I don't know' to the question, 'Is there a God?' And this really does describe me. I really don't know. Religious people with faith know for certain there's a God. On the other side are the fundamentalist scientists – and there are a lot of them around these days – who say, 'We know there's no such thing as a god. Science can explain the whole universe. It's a material that's just happened by itself. There's no being out there that's designed anything or made anything. There is no god.' I think that position is too extreme, and I'm in the middle; it's a very broad, open middle ground, and we agnostics occupy it.

A lot of people would be surprised, because you've devoted your life to the study of observable fact, of data. And yet at this crucial point you say, 'I actually don't know the answer.'

Well, it's rather like the reply given by a very distinguished physicist to the question, 'Do you believe in flying saucers?' He answered, 'I think it's very improbable that they exist.' He didn't say, 'No, I don't believe in them, it's a lot of rubbish.' Neither did he say, 'Yes, they may be. I think there's a chance.' He just said it's very improbable, and this is the same view I have about the question, 'Is there a god?' I certainly never, even from my childhood, believed in the idea of a bearded old gentleman sitting up there in the sky, looking down and watching everything, giving me a sense of guilt. But I don't believe in any kind of human-form designer of the universe. Voltaire's notion that 'Man made God in his own image' is so true. We make models of the world around us, and we make models of God. But in the case of the world around us, we can match our models with the observable nature. As far as God goes, that's something way out we can't match at all. It doesn't mean he doesn't exist, or it doesn't exist, but we can't know it. We can't say anything about it. So it's best to be an agnostic.

You mentioned your childhood. I'd like to trace the source of doubt. Was your family agnostic, or were you brought up with any faith at all?

My mother was a Quaker. It's probably the most sceptical religion of the whole lot. At the particular Meeting that I attended as a child – which was in Brixton in south London – they didn't go much for the Bible at all, particularly not the Old Testament. They tended to go more by two books the Quakers had, called the Books of Discipline, which were mainly accounts of early Quakers dealing with problems, usually humanist problems of imprisonment and so on. So in a sense I was brought up in an atmosphere of rational scepticism rather than religious faith.

You wrote that your father used to rescue wasps because he said they had their purpose in the universe. Do you think that's where your own fascination with the grand design of the universe began?

'Grand design of the universe' is too big a term, really. My father was much more down to earth. From childhood he was fascinated by the natural world – a kind of homespun ecologist, if you like. He was a very keen gardener and he knew the wasps went for the plums, but he also knew that wasps spent a lot of their time as predators on some of the more damaging insects that would damage the plants, so he felt that a proper balance required keeping the wasps, not going out and destroying them. As a child, I was given this background information about nature, that integrated into the pleasant experience of a walk in the country – going out and enjoying it. It all became an integral part of my brain, of my life. I think without my father's teaching I probably wouldn't have developed a theory like Gaia.

At this stage we ought to define what that is. Can you just put it simply, because I know it's a very complex theory?

Gaia theory sees the earth as a complete system made up of all the living things – all of them, from bacteria all the way up to whales, from tiny algae living in the ocean all the way up to giant redwood trees, and all of the great ecosystems of the forests and so on. All of that life part is not alone but tightly integrated with the atmosphere, the ocean and the surface rocks. And the whole of that constitutes a single system that regulates itself, keeps the climate constant and comfortable for life, keeps the chemical composition of the atmosphere so that it's always breathable. There's always the right amount of oxygen in the air. It's very important it should be the right amount. If there were just a few per cent more, fires would be so fierce that all of the forests would be burned down. If there were less, there would be no forest fires, and this would upset the ecology of the earth because it depends on them. So it's a system that regulates itself quite accurately. That's all it is.

I used the phrase 'grand design' before, which you said was too large a term. But hearing you describe Gaia – which, of course, is the name of the Greek earth goddess – that does sound like a grand design. Now when you first propounded this theory at the beginning of the 1970s, end of the 1960s, a lot of scientists dismissed it because they said it was teleological, implying purpose, implying a designing god. Is that right?

Absolutely, and it's very interesting that you should have said it seems like a grand design. That's just what they thought – but I wasn't saying anything of the kind. I was saying it's a system that evolved automatically, without any purpose, foresight or anything. It just happened and has been in existence now for about three and a half to four billion years. A very tough system . . .

In a way, you were ahead of your time, in seeing the wholeness of things. The word 'holistic' is used a lot now. But there's a sense in which you were only expressing a knowledge which people have had for centuries. You know, there's that Green Man figure which appears on Christian churches – a pagan symbol. But there was a belief in the essential unity of things even then.

Oh, I think so. It goes all the way back. I'm sure when men and women could first think about the world around them, they were bound to have wondered if it was something that was almost alive. I know my biological colleagues are always jumping on me when I imply even that the earth is alive. I don't mean alive like an animal. What I am implying is alive in the sense of being able to regulate itself – in the way that you keep your temperature always at 37°C, except when you have a fever or when you're dead. It's the same with the earth. It's always kept its temperature close on to where we are at the moment – not far off 20°C, a bit below it at the moment. It was a bit above it in past epochs. But during all the time that there's been life on the earth, the sun has increased its output of heat by 25 per cent. And so it's a remarkable thing that it's always kept constant. It's like a person going from living in the Arctic to living in the tropics. You keep your temperature constant because you're alive. So does the earth . . .

Do you think one of the problems for 'modern man in search of a soul' – the name of a book by Jung – is that in fact the discoveries of science have left the rest of us in ignorance and without God? God has been banished from our horizon and there is nothing to take his place.

It's not that the scientific approach is bad and it's taken God away from us and given us nothing. I think the scientific approach is wholly good. It spins off from a sense of wonder – and wonder, after all, is what it's all about in its origins. If you have a hypothesis there's a god, that's only one hypothesis, and it may not be right. There are others, and looking at it scientifically you keep an open mind until you have so much evidence that it's overwhelming and you are fairly sure you can believe in something. I think what's happened is that scientists have betrayed science, rather than that the method itself is wrong. Since science became a career, a job where you went to from nine to five, with employment status and a pension, it has lost its soul altogether. Science is a vocation, like the arts. Can you imagine an institute of fine art where painters went along every day and clocked in to do their painting? The whole thing's absurd, but we expect science to go on that way . . .

Does it surprise you that throughout the centuries, millions and millions of people, in every culture you can imagine – from the primitive to the most highly sophisticated – have required God?

Yes, it does make me wonder because I don't really know the answer, and I don't think anybody does.

So you don't really understand that need?

I would acknowledge that it's there, and that for me it's fully satisfied by a sense of wonder about the universe. I've no depression at all associated with 'There is no God. Why am I here? It's all pointless. It's all automatic. I'm just a thing that's going to terminate in not too long a time . . .' It's never bothered me.

One of the great weaknesses of modern life is we're all structured to think of time. We don't live for the minute, as primitive people do . . . I think modern life makes people value tenure, value their insurance policies and all of that kind of thing, and that is what makes them so miserable. They are reminded every day that life is finite.

If, in all your studies of the life of the earth, you rejected the idea of the purpose being that of God, what about a universal spirit of nature – the kind of thing Wordsworth and Coleridge celebrated? The idea of a life force running through all things?

I think that's woolly liberalism, to be quite honest. I think it's more honest to have a monotheistic god up there as a postulate. It's a little more testable than this vague universal spirit of nature. I know what they're on about. It's a kind of lovely warm feeling you get when you go out on a nice sunny morning and hear the birds singing and smell all the may trees – the freshness of it all. You're bound to get feelings which many people would call religious or something. I don't feel any need to do that. I'm quite happy to enjoy it. I don't want to explain it.

I'm going to have to defend them here, because I think it was slightly more than appreciating the prettiness of trees. It was seeing nature as a moral force, as when King Lear shouts, 'Hear, Nature! Hear, Great Goddess, hear!' And that doesn't seem to me to be far removed from your theories of Gaia, which requires of us a moral sense about the universe.

No. Your point's very well taken. Indeed, you can use Gaia as a kind of moral metaphor. The nature of the world system is strangely like the attributes given to the ancient goddess Gaia or the Indian goddess Kali. They were both of them feminine, kindly, nurturing, but also quite ruthless towards transgressors. Kali drank the blood of humans from a skull. And if we go on messing about with the planet, it may well be metaphorically our fate. The rules of the game in Gaia are that if you live well with the world and the environment, and if you tend to improve it, your progeny will flourish. If, on the other hand, you pollute it, corrupt it in any way, then the Gaia view is that you will be eliminated because your progeny will not succeed so well.

It seems to me that the organised religions of the world and the kind of pantheism which was felt by Wordsworth and Coleridge and your kind of science have one thing in common, which is the awareness of the need for humility.

Absolutely, and one of my main quarrels with modern science is that it has the opposite of humility: hubris, overweening pride. It goes right across the board. You will find many a physicist nowadays who, if you interview him or speak with him, will give you the impression that yesterday he was speaking to God, and this is what God said . . . ! And you'll find biologists, likewise, who will come out with statements saying, 'Science can explain everything.' This shows a total absence of humility, and makes us fail to understand that we are a fairly lately evolved animal on the earth – just an animal, along with all the other animals. We're not that clever. We should wonder, for example, what on earth the great whales, with their brains ten times as large as ours and full of functional cells, are doing. They may be much more brilliant than we are.

Do you reject humanism as a philosophy?

Very much so. I think it's a self-limiting and self-destructive philosophy. Unless we recognise that we are part of a great community of organisms that make up this system Gaia – assuming that it's a fair description of the earth – we will tend to do things which are good for people only. And if we do that, then people will die. The rules of the Gaia game are: you must look after the earth. If you don't do that, then the earth will take care of you, eliminate you from the scene. It will always take care of itself, and we will pay the price. So humanism is a self-defeating philosophy.

You use the term 'animal' to describe us, and obviously we are animals. Does, then, the word 'soul' have any meaning for you?

Very much so. I'm not going to define it because my feelings are a scientific intuition that there is a state in the mind which corresponds to many of the other ideas of the soul, but it's no more than a mental state. The only analogy I can give you is a modern one:

that is, when you have a computer on your desk and it's switched on and there's nothing in it, there's no programmes, there's nothing working – it's alive in an electrical sense, it's switched on and functioning. But when it has a programme running in it, there's nothing that you could measure has been added to it. You couldn't weigh it, the existence of it, but it is something that is there in the idea space of the computer that is an entity in its own right. It's such an entity, it can even be attacked by viruses, as you probably know. I like to think of the soul as a similar class of entity within the idea space that the hardware of the brain constitutes. So I am not at all unhappy with the idea of the soul, although it may be very different from the concept of the soul held by many a theologian or religious person . . .

. . . The only way to live is for *now*. Many of the great religions, of course, give this as advice: 'Take no thought for the morrow . . . Consider the lilies – they toil not, neither do they spin.' It's not a new idea. It's an old one.

As a scientist I support myself by being an inventor. I don't really separate the two. Now this makes me a very practical person. Once a subject in my opinion is ineffable (to use a theological term), unknowable – like 'What was the origin of the universe?' 'What were the origins of life?' – it doesn't fascinate me at all because there's no evidence available. There's hardly anything you can get your hands on to wonder about, so to speak. I'm much more interested in the earth here and now. It's full of stuff you can get at and go and measure and start to understand, and yet still full of wonder – much more important than the origins of the universe. Those are, to use a term that turns it round, theological questions that scientists should not be asking. But it's a wonderful world, an astonishing universe, and, to quote a lovely remark from that strange old scientist and atheist J.B.S. Haldane: 'The universe is not only mysterious: it's far more mysterious than you'll ever be able to imagine.' That really encapsulates all, I think.

(1993 conversation)

Edna O'Brien

Novelist, screenwriter and playwright Edna O'Brien caused a sensation with *The Country Girls* in 1960 and since then has published many novels and short stories, gaining a considerable following at home and abroad. She recently adapted the *Iphigenia* of Sophocles for the Crucible Theatre, Sheffield.

Many of the facts of your life are well known: the fact that you were educated in a convent, your Irish Catholic background. Can I ask you first if you were ever 'in love' with God?

Oh yes, utterly. I think, to this day perhaps, I mix up secular love and spiritual love. One was fed, so to speak, on God, the presence of God. All over the house were holy pictures, particularly the Sacred Heart, and I so identified with this – forgive the morbidity – 'bleeding heart' because there was a little lamp in front of it and this Semite face with long dark hair enthralled me. I was in love with God in two ways: one was to suffer on his behalf, and the other was to be espoused to him . . . This love was no doubt a very masochistic and Irish Catholic kind of love, but it sustained me. There was a great loving – not forgiving, but loving – deity whom I could appeal to and be with. And although I don't feel it in the same way, there's a lingering residue of that. My love of God – although it has suffered some setbacks, if not to say some quarrels, over the years – still resides in me because of the child in me, the child that is in us all . . .

So with all that background, the intensity at home and school, at what point did you start to rebel against it, and was that rebellion against the personal God or the God of dogma?

I had told my favourite nun I was going to be a nun. I was a bit in love with her. And I began to fast and pray even more than normal. I was always fasting, always praying, gargling with salt and water to purify myself for God. I came home for the long summer holiday, and I had never really gone to dances or anything because I thought it was wrong. I thought everything to do with romance and sex – this was at fifteen or sixteen years of age – was sinful.

But I went to a dance and met somebody and had a kiss, not on the dance floor but outside the hall in the secrecy of the dark – just a kiss. And it was so exciting and so ecstatic that when I went back in and danced with this man I realised, of course, that I had betrayed my soul. I had sinned against God and against my vow of a vocation.

I didn't become a nun, and I forget how I slithered out of it but I saw that there had to be a choice between wanting the kiss or remaining faithful and chaste. I have had very few love affairs, for the record! So it wasn't an intellectual departure, it wasn't founded on anything, only fear – the fear that I had transgressed.

For instance, to go to confession, there were two primary conditions otherwise the confession was null and void: you had to be truly sorry for your sin and you had to have what is called 'purpose of amendment' – the certainty that you would never commit that sin again. Now I thought, 'I can't go to confession and say that if I don't mean it, because am I never going to kiss anyone in my life again?' Therefore I stopped going, even though I saw a lot of people around me who sallied off to confession and the next night were in the fields with someone. But I couldn't. I thought it was a greater sin, you see, to lie to oneself. So I left the Church –

still went, of course, and did a bit of genuflection and put a lot of money in St Anthony's box for favours, and said prayers and asked for forgiveness, but I didn't go to Holy Communion – couldn't . . .

I parted abruptly and angrily from the God that the Catholic Church imposed upon me. I believe now that I had – and maybe still have – as much faith and as much spiritual hunger as my indoctrinators. And it was only as time went on that I began to see that, throughout history, throughout time, throughout the ages, fundamental to a great number of people, is this craving for God, and a God that shows mercy, because nobody's life is that happy, even those who pretend it is. The idea that there is something *other* is very important. I think now that I do believe – and *want* to believe – in a God, even though I have to question, as any sensible human being would, the enormity, barbarity, injustice, insanity and ongoing murderousness in the world around us. You look at television and see dazed, starving children in Africa trying to pick the flies from their eyelids and you think, 'Are all these created by the same God, and for what reason?' To die of starvation aged six weeks or six months is monstrous.

When you lost faith in the Church and God, was it terrifying? Did you feel really alone – like a parent's hand gone away? Because obviously you needed that structure.

I felt not only alone, but something worse – I felt a terror, because you never escape the vivid sermons regarding hell and purgatory. We all know it would be physically impossible to accommodate the number of people in any of the four places – limbo can't be left out – but I was very afraid that I would, literally, end up in eternal writhing flames. But at the same time, you know how it is with fears like that – you somehow repress them. You're not thinking of them every minute, but you're thinking of them in the fallow hours, in times of crisis, times of loss.

 . . . In the Buddhist teaching, in the scripture of the yogis, they talk of the god inside one, and if we were to consciously keep that in mind we would be much more caring, we would be much more truthful, we would be much holier. It wouldn't be someone else telling us, it would be us, acknowledging that divine or spiritual seed within ourselves. It is true that the early world in Ireland I described isn't so relevant, but what is sad is that by losing the faith in the existence of God, a lot of people have also lost some of their decency, their morality, their conscience.

So they needed the framework?

I really do think so. Again, it's a question of balance. You might say to me, 'Would you recommend to people in Ireland that they went through the experiences you went through vis-à-vis the Church?' and I would say, 'No, I couldn't, because it's a rope around the neck. It's strangulation.' But I would instil in people just to be open to the idea of God, the presence of a divinity in the self and the good things that faith can do . . .

At what sort of times do you pray, actually turn to the God you said you had been unfaithful to?

It can be anywhere, but especially when life is dark and one is broken, then instinctively one turns to prayer, one cries out.

So when you pray to him or her or it, do you think that there's a listener there?

I'm not sure. I'm not sure. How could I be? I think if you live in Bosnia or if you live in Belfast or if you live in Somalia or Ethiopia – whatever your admitted faith or non-faith is – it is hard to believe you are being heard by a good God. Yet people do go on praying, because they have to. It's like breaking down walls or battering on the door of the unknown.

I had a very strange dream once in which I saw God, and it was a sort of prophetic dream, a final battle, between people of the Muslim faith and the Jewish faith. It was a very terrible dream. The weapons were not guns or grenades, they were humans – human blood wrapped in human flesh to become the next missile. I was in Battalion Three, waiting to go, and as the first battalion came off they were being severed to serve as weapons for us, and I saw it so clearly and so distinctly – to this day it freaks me. I saw God and he spoke. He said, 'It is not for earthly considerations you fight, you suffer so, it is to catch sight of God.' Well now, the Catholic Church would have been very proud of me. They would have said, 'She may have strayed but she wasn't able to renounce him.' It was a shocking dream in all its detail, and also in the idea of God asking of humans such a brutal sacrifice.

. . . You've always been divided. You've written that the idea of the divided psyche is always fascinating to you. But you intimated a little bit earlier that you're coming round again . . .

I think everybody rebels in their youth, either politically or socially or religiously, because it's a natural thing to rebel against authority, against parents, but if I am returning it is to a different God, not the one I was brought up on, first fed on.

What's he like?

Well, I hope that he has compassion and forgiveness in his heart – I'm speaking now just totally subjectively – I hope that he is a guardian to me. It's a very audacious thing to say, but I also hope he's really intelligent, because if somebody is really intelligent then they understand everything, don't they? Intelligence is the key to knowing and seeing into another person's predicament without being judgmental. I'd like God to be sublimely intelligent, as well as sublimely tender.

(1993 conversation)

Ben Okri

The poet and novelist won the Booker Prize in 1991 for *The Famished Road*, and since then has won international acclaim for novels which include *Songs of Enchantment* (1993), *Dangerous Love* (1996), *Infinite Riches* (1998), and *Arcadi* (2002). He has published a collection of essays, and marked the millennium with *Mental Fight*, an inspiring sequence of poems.

You were born in Nigeria and came to England as a baby. Then you went back, rather unwillingly, as a small boy. Then you came back to England as a young man. So you journeyed between two continents, two cultures, two world views, and maybe very different attitudes to religion. Can you talk a little bit about those contrasts?

A journey from Nigeria to Britain as a child has a profound effect on you for ever afterwards. I don't know which is more profound in the effect, the journey here or the journey back. They each had a deep spiritual impact on the way I think, write and live.

I was born in the north of Nigeria. That's where we were living at the time. But my father and mother are from the mid-west of

Nigeria. I came to London around the age of about a year and a half. I was here till about seven. While here, I lived, in spiritual terms, on three levels. School and its religious education. My parents' traditional and religious beliefs. And then there was the world of my childhood, my reading and my thinking.

What were your parents' beliefs?

They attended an African Christian church. African Christianity tends to be eclectic. They sometimes have the ritual quality of Catholicism as well as the austerity of the Protestant Church. I am at ease in both of these different manifestations of Western Christianity.

My own form of spirituality is different from religion. One has got to do with an institution, and the other with the self's quest for the highest meaning that life can offer. It's also quite eclectic and has to do with travelling between cultures. A sort of spiritual relativity became aware that the African way alone does not describe all of life and all of life's possibilities. And the British way, the Christian way alone, does not do that either. Each world view seems to work for the different peoples. This therefore made me open myself up to other religions and to other spiritual ways like Buddhism, Taoism, Hinduism. I took an interest in all of these Eastern forms. Much later on I took an interest in some aspects of Judaism, and Islam, because I found that something runs through all of them and they all resonate with one another.

In The Famished Road, *which won the Booker Prize, and then following it,* Songs of Enchantment *and* Infinite Riches, *we follow the story of Azario , the spirit child. Can you just explain the idea of the spirit child?*

Well, first of all it's important to stress that the whole idea of the spirit child is one that I have bent myself. It is a poetic inflection of what is known in many African traditions, but it is particularly famous among the Yoruba and the Ibo peoples. It's just simply a child that keeps being born and keeps returning to the land before birth, and is compelled to come back again. They don't like the conditions they find in the world into which they're born. They can will their deaths. They go back. They leave. Some can be charmed from this condition so that they don't actually go back, they don't die . . .

The implication of the spirit child seems to me to be quite profound. Apart from the hint of reincarnation, there is the level of responsibility involved in making the world worthwhile for children to want to stay in, to want to live in, to want to grow up in and to which they can contribute. The spirit child is one of the greatest criticisms of life as we have made it. They pass judgment on the world by refusing to deal with it, because they say, 'You've made a mess of it. I don't want to stay.' All I was trying to do was to present an enormous paradox. There's a paradox and tension. There's a tension between a world that is extremely difficult for children to grow up in, to want to grow up in, and one which they've fallen in love with for some complex and mysterious reason. You see, these novels forced me to have to find the simple, superficial and the deeper reasons why one would want to live. That requires great energy, requires a great sense of regeneration, a great sense of looking at everything in the world again with new and fresh eyes.

Coming from the life that I'd lived, and writing about Africa, it seemed to me absolutely essential that the spirit child not be a tragic figure, which is what the spirit child is normally perceived as. Because they're going to leave: they're going to go any minute. I wanted to reinvent and reinvigorate and regenerate that figure in our consciousness, because by doing that, the life itself gets transformed and regenerated. And then we can begin the whole process of transforming our reality.

At times of great pain in your own life, where do you seek comfort?

That's a very difficult question. It's very hard to know where to seek comfort when great pain, great tragedy falls upon you, because it tends to turn your world upside down, it bursts it wide open. All the certainties that you had, and all the places that you had that you thought could help you, don't. And many, many things are exposed for not being deep enough in the way they were meant to help us cope with the extremes and the vicissitudes of the human experience.

When my mother died, for example – I prefer the words 'passed on', 'moved on' – it was such an appalling experience, an appalling moment in my life. It was like there's an earth inside the soul, inside the spirit – not an earth underneath your feet, but an earth inside of you. It gets taken away completely and you're standing absolutely on air, on nothing. And all the walls around your emotions, and all the walls around your skin: it's as though everything has gone and a hole so huge opens up inside you. Everything that you are – your identity – goes right out through it. It's quite the most emptying experience I have ever been through. I remember at the time finding myself actually having to hold on to solid things like walls and lamp-posts, and found that they weren't solid enough. I'd lean against a tree and find it wasn't solid enough. I used to go to the gym around that time, and I just didn't have the strength to even so much as walk on the treadmill. Every single ounce of energy in my being had drained out completely. All the physical things, all the things that we turn to for sustenance and support, I found to be quite hopeless and quite empty.

What it actually did was make me ask questions again about the true sustainers of the human spirit. What is it that, when these things befall us, we can rely on, turn to? And it's a really difficult question, it really, really is. It stripped me apart utterly, and it began a new and important journey in my spiritual and intellectual life, in a way. The religious structures, church, helped, but not as deeply as I thought it would, and this is a terrible thing to have to say. The reason is because at the time, I experienced something very peculiar. I realised that the pastor, the priest who was speaking to me at the time about my grief, spoke to me from the book but not from the experience, so he could not speak to the grief in me. He couldn't speak to the emptiness in me because, at the time, he hadn't gone through it himself. I can say this now with a certain amount of tranquillity, because about four years later his mother died and he wrote to me and said, 'Oh my goodness. I didn't know. *That's* what you were going through at the time.'

That's part of the problem. How can we speak to the deep things in one another if we haven't been through them ourselves and if the structures that are there don't have practices? I think nothing short of some embraceable practice can help us through them. I don't think just sitting in a building of whatever kind, alone in prayer, can do it. I've found when I'm speaking to people, they tend to have two or three sets of ways of coping with deep experiences. One is work. They hide themselves in work. They just work and work and work and work, till the wound as they perceive it has been, as it were, barked over. I am not comfortable with that at all. There's the other that says, 'Throw yourself into society. Go out often. Be out among people. Do charitable work, immerse yourself in other people's suffering.' That's good, that's beautiful, and that transforms your suffering into something of value to other people, and I think it raises something in you.

Then there's another. That is, I think, finding ways to reconnect, for want of a better word, with that mysterious thing that is higher than all of us and that we all partake in. Some traditions speak of it as forms of meditation, forms of a very profound kind of prayer. In other words, I'm speaking of practice. I think what is missing is some kind of spiritual *practice* in our lives. It's just like everything else. If you want to develop certain skills, you have to do certain practices. If it's the martial arts, for example, you have to do your *katas* and so on. If it's dancing, you have to go through those movements. I think the same thing is true of spiritual matters as well.

So in the months, and indeed years, following this intense grief, did you attempt to evolve such a practice for yourself?

I think it sent me on a quest. Because I had to answer that question. I couldn't continue without answering it. It was as simple as that. So it started me on a search and a quest.

Was the question to find a meaning in the loss of your mother, and how to absorb that into yourself?

The loss of our mum in itself was a huge thing, because of the love and the specific fact of one's mother having gone. All of that grief and pain. But it also exposed something enormous, I think, that we all carry around in us and that we are covering up most of the time – which is that one is living more or less blindly, we're not as solid as we think we are, we're not as held together as we think we are. The ropes and tricks and thoughts and . . . achievements, etc., by which we wrap up our perception of ourselves and prop up our egos, and present ourselves to the world . . . actually, they're just nothing. They're illusions. They're just dust. They're constructions. I have known people . . . the loss of their child has completely just emptied, devastated and torn apart everything. It didn't make them lose all their money in the bank. It didn't make them lose their positions or their places in society. It didn't do anything like that. What it did was, it went to the very core of their being, the very centre of who they are. It led them to some impossible mystery. I think the person is revealed in how they cope with that, and that's what fascinates me.

And has it changed for you? Has it evolved?

I think it's changed me enormously. I don't know if it's visible on the outside. I don't care. It's not important to me that it be visible – probably best if it's not. Inside, yes, it has brought about the beginnings of very important transformations. I have had to ask myself what the fundamental things are. I've had to take away the power that one's given to certain aspects of life . . . and find that which one thinks *is* important, more enduring, more of a sustained value which may be able to help one through this great business of living.

Is it possible for you to hazard a definition of what you're left with when you've got rid of all the other things?

I think we all pretty well know what these things are. Actually, we've been told them from childhood. We've heard these things a thousand times before. It's just that we've not invested them with the intensity of truth that they deserve. I can quote to you texts from Buddhism, from Islam, all the great religions – passages that say the same thing. In Christianity it says, 'Of what value is it to you if you gain the whole world, but lose your soul?' There's another passage where it hints at the fact that the things that you have are not the most enduring things. The parables of different religions speak of caskets that are of gold and inside they have nothing, and caskets that are of lead and inside them there is the true gold. There are hints here and there in all sorts of mystical traditions that tell us that our great visible accomplishments are not where our real accomplishments are. That may be our more invisible accomplishments, charity, love, courage, service to our fellow human beings – not in a boring sort of way, but a service rendered because we feel connected. That profound concern for the globe, this earth that we live on: all of these things. It is not what one accomplishes in oneself; I think it is what one accomplishes for all of humanity . . .

Around the millennium you published a sequence of poems called Mental Fight *about where we are, where we might be going, which was very uplifting and very positive in its analysis. But in it you seem to suggest at one point that human beings can follow too many gods. And you go on: 'We know only two kinds of response to the unknown: awe or noise.' And then 'Prayer or panic', which I thought was very interesting because a lot of people do what one might call scrabble around in astrology and feng shui and all these different beliefs. Is your response ever panic – to all the responsibility and all the possibilities?*

If one is honest, I think being alive and being human is a somewhat panicky condition. To affect complete certainty about life is to not be richly aware of what it is to be human. Because we don't have that much control over the factors that surround our lives at all. We have absolutely no way of dealing with death. Forget science here . . . It's against this that we must begin to find a new form, a new way, a new dimension and a new quest. That's where humility starts. That's where philosophy starts, real philosophy, private philosophy, the one by which we either cope or we don't.

I'll just pick up this idea of the quest and the destination . . . Some years ago you made one of those BBC television programmes, Great Railway Journeys, *and you chose Arcadia, and this provides the framework, just the starting point, for your latest novel. But Arcadia doesn't exist. So how can you travel somewhere that doesn't exist?*

Well, it exists and it doesn't exist. The journey to a place that doesn't exist is really a quest for an answer to some of the questions that we've been raising throughout our discussion. I don't think it's totally possible to live a vaguely meaningful life without actually asking and trying to come to terms with these questions. I don't think it's possible. Socrates said it pretty simply: 'The unexamined life is not worth living.' He's right. That's what the journey to Arcadia is. And this novel is not really about that journey, but is actually an examination in fictional terms of 'How do we cope with the anxiety of living?'

It's a journey from a place to another place, meeting people along the way, and all these characters change during that journey, especially the narrator. But it's also a journey from darkness to light, isn't it?

From darkness to a less darkness, I think, is the best way of putting it . . .
  . . . The novel begins with anxiety, because all journeys begin with anxiety. It's only great anxiety and crisis that sets us off travelling and asking questions; that sets us out of our homes and making great journeys to different lands – sometimes in books, sometimes through other people, sometimes in religions. Quests and asking questions . . . it's an anxiety, it's a great distress. It's a terminal condition in which we see the world around us – the threats of environmental collapse, the famines that scream all over the world, the deadness and deafness of our conscience to the innumerable ways that people suffer and die and perish on this globe. Anyone who gets away from it – it's only because they're refusing to see it. It's there. And the only way through something like that is to acknowledge the fact that we are living in the world that we've created, which is fringed with and becoming

increasingly enriched with unacceptable disasters. We have to face that fact, and we have to travel through that fact. And that's the only form of responsibility there is: the clarity of seeing this, accepting it, and travelling through it with our eyes wide open and our senses wide awake and saying that we are human beings. Humanity is not going to perish. We're going to have to deal with this thing and take these problems by the horn and make something of this globe before it disappears and disintegrates into a great big ugly bowl of soup.

But do you have faith that, given all the proof to the contrary, we can do this?

I wouldn't use the word 'faith'. There is something in us that is greater than the darkness that we have created ourselves. There is some magic ingredient in us. One aspect of it is humour. We love to laugh, and once the spirit laughs, we've already started to dissolve the darkness. We have an incredible capacity for cheerfulness in the face of such ugliness and such distress. It's unbelievable. You go to places in Africa and India where people suffer the most. You see the folks are cheerful. They sing. Some Westerners find this appalling and think they couldn't do that, but you can't measure the human spirit. The depths are astonishing. The other thing is the quality of surprise. There's just no telling with humanity. There just really isn't. We begin to show our greatest strength when we're faced with our greatest disasters, in a way.

There's just something charming and enchanting about the human spirit, in spite of our great negativity and fantastical laziness and indifference. There's also this mysterious thing called love. I don't know: we may be really crooked and awkward and corrupt, and we mess things up. But once we fall in love with somebody, an idea, an act, that love itself suddenly makes us see the world differently, and makes us roll our sleeves up and say, 'OK, we're going to clear up this mess.' It's amazing what people do when they fall in love. So we've got so many things inside us as part of our make-up. I think what is just needed is for those wonder elements in us to be touched, those springs of regeneration to be awoken, and humanity will do the rest itself, because it has the strength and the will and the desire to do that. Humanity does not fundamentally want to perish.

(2002 conversation)

Susie Orbach

Susie Orbach is arguably the best-known psychotherapist in Britain. Born in 1946 and educated in London and New York, she has also distinguished herself as a columnist and broadcaster. In 1976 she co-founded the Women's Therapy Centre in London and in 1981 the Women's Therapy Centre Institute in New York. Since *Fat is a Feminist Issue* (1976) she has published many other books including *The Impossibility of Sex* (2002).

. . . Well, that brings me to this paragraph that I wanted to read to you in The Impossibility of Sex *which struck me because of the feelings behind it. 'The psychotherapist who is faced with hearing the detailed stories of human suffering and the cruelties that can be perpetrated between people cannot run away. It is her job to listen. She has to find a way to hear what is being spoken of, to bear witness to the perverse, the sadistic, the barbarous and the unimaginable. In this she is aided both by the skills developed in training to listen, feel and hear without becoming overwhelmed and by the theoretical frameworks available for thinking about the gruesome material that enters the consulting room.'*

I wondered what strategies you used beyond the theoretical framework,

*because you're a very intelligent and rounded person, and to me it seems
like the theoretical framework can't be enough.*

No, I don't think the theoretical framework is enough. One thing is
that when you're in the therapy room, which is a contained amount
of time, it's fifty minutes, and you are there for the other, you're
there thinking with the other. You absorb an awful lot of information, and painful and cruel material and sometimes gruesome, and
unlike in normal social conversation you don't just react back, you
don't send the ball back, you absorb it and then you get to think
about it. So you reposition this stuff inside of yourself, if I can put
it like that. You develop a curiosity towards the most painful or the
most gruesome or the most heart-wrenching activities that people
have either experienced or perpetrated, and you also feel the pain of
those events with them. You don't deny the pain of those events,
because, actually, you couldn't be a therapist if you did. Your own
response, your own subjectivity, which you may or may not share
with them, forms the way that you absorb what happens in the
room. I mean, it's not possible to hear about anything from a cot
death to somebody perpetrating sexual abuse, let's say, or bullying
somebody, without feeling a sense of pain, fright, terror or anxiety.
All of those things you feel inside of yourself while you're sitting
with somebody. But what you don't do is react with 'How could
you do that?'

Have you ever treated anybody whom you have felt to be evil?

That's such a good question, because I think that what psychoanalysis does is . . . it deconstructs behaviours and actions on the
part of people, so that it tends to find the humanity in them. So evil
might be my initial emotional response, but I'm not sure that I
would ever be held in that place in my mind about the person. I
might then see their evilness – this is not to let them off the hook –
but I might see it as part of the defence structure they developed
because of certain circumstances in their lives.

Sinned against as well as sinning?

Yes, absolutely.

When you were young, was there a specific point when you thought, 'Yes, I can make sense of things'?

Oh, I think I thought that all along, from teenage on, but not particularly in terms of psychoanalysis. I mean, I thought it in terms of history or in terms of politics or economics and thought it in terms of feminism. So I think making sense was something I always wanted to do, whether it was making sense of space or relationships or social class or something aesthetic . . . Maybe it implies a wish to be able to put things within a framework. I don't know whether you'd say that was from being out of control or whether it's because I wouldn't know how to understand something without some kind of conceptual markers.

Did that process and the search for solutions ever incorporate a need for a personal religious faith?

No. I think I had one week of going to every church and synagogue – there weren't really any mosques in London where I grew up – when I was about twelve. I think that was my religious faith. But I come from a secular Jewish background where the secular and the Jewish went together in a very strong way, and it would have been inconceivable for me to have thought of a god as being anything rather than a kind of historic phenomenon for the people that I came from.

Did you attend synagogue when you were small?

Not at all. I was sent to Sunday school for a short time but I think that was a rather hopeless endeavour on the part of my parents. I think they probably wanted me to get some of the stories. I wasn't getting the Christian stories because Jewish girls didn't go into Christian prayers, and I think they didn't want me to be culturally disadvantaged, but I don't think I absorbed them terribly well.

So there was secular Judaism and a sense of cultural history. Did you find that a rich mix?

Well, it wasn't exceptional. There was a whole trajectory of post-war Jews who were in the first generation of Jews who wanted to raise their children in a secular fashion and who lived a secular life. They had politics. What it meant to be a Jew for them was more to do with social justice, was to do with fighting for peace, for equality, against racism. It had absolutely nothing to do with God, although there were a couple of festivals that were celebrated for the meanings associated with the historical struggles of the Jews, but they weren't meant to be privileged over other struggles of other people, I suppose . . .

. . . I did go and live in New York in my early twenties, and that's a sort of Jewish/Black/Latin/Irish/Italian city where everybody's ethnicity and cultural background was really strong, and so I didn't have to reject the Jewish secular thing because it was right there – it was part of what New York offered me, in fact. What was I going to reject? One understood that anti-Semitism and racism were terrible and that actually you had to be a Jew as long as those things existed . . . that it's absolutely critical that one identifies oneself as a Jew as long as racism exists because otherwise it's whitewashing racism. It's saying, 'We don't have to deal with this.' So I didn't really need to fight against that in some way, and even when I was studying history there were progressive Zionist struggles at the turn of the last century which I could fit myself into politically and think about. So I didn't really need to reject the Jewish bit.

What about your life now? For a lot of people as they get older, one is drawn to think – perhaps through an experience like a bereavement – about matters of life and death and why we're here and where we're going. Do you find now that you have brought into your adulthood, your maturity, anything from the cultural background, the Judaism that you were nearly brought up with?

Well, I think you want me to find a little hole in me that has religion in it . . .

. . . the God-shaped hole . . .

. . . and I'm afraid that it doesn't really exist. I suppose the older I get the more wondrous the world seems to me, and the more profound the fact of our existence is as a species, and the more interesting to me. And the more I am prepared to recognise that – I don't know. I don't mean about religion, but simply the origins of the universe, which is so extraordinary, and the fact that people achieve the things they do, is so moving to me. I kind of have a spiritual peace which doesn't have religion associated with it, and as I age I feel just moved and . . . in wonder.

At the mystery of things and what humanity can do?

Yes. I mean, it's the extraordinary nature of our capacity both to co-operate and create beautiful things, relationships, aesthetics, objects that transform our lives, but it's also the cruelties that I think we're capable of which are also extraordinary, and it's our ways of ignoring the natural world and the ways in which we can engage with the natural world. So I'm staggered by all of these things. And, of course, in my practice I work with a lot of people who do hold very deep religious beliefs. It's not that I'm exempt from being forced to think about them and the ways in which they are very holding influences or frameworks for other people, it's just that it seems to me that the world is so rich in and of itself that I don't need something called God to do it for me.

In The Impossibility of Sex *you use two phrases which I really like: 'the psychic debris' and 'the inner wasteland'. And obviously the people who come to you do so because they have psychic debris. So is it frequent in your consulting room for God to come as the other person there?*

I don't think that's how it happens. I think that people come to therapy with tremendous shame and distress about the difficulties that they're in. If they happen to be of strong religious belief then they feel even more humiliated that they haven't been able to achieve what their religion holds up for them, that they've failed in some sense to make a meaningful life, given everything they believe in.

But I don't think God comes in . . . I don't think people say, 'Well, I suppose this is what we call God.' She or he might be thinking, 'This is what I call God,' and I might be thinking, 'Well, this is what I call connection in a relationship,' but I don't think it walks in in quite the way that you're imagining.

. . . I don't think self-involvement and self-awareness exempt you or remove you from deep spiritual connection with the world or with others. I don't experience that in my patients or the people I'm working with at all – in fact, I think, through the process of therapy, those who have needed it have come to feel much more connected to others and are much more creative as a result of their experiences in therapy.

. . . Actually not hiding from but confronting some of the helplessness we have to feel as human beings – that's something we have to come to terms with at some point in life. Not that we have no control, but that there are moments when actually things are capricious or terrible things happen or very painful things happen, and we are not in a position to transform everything and sometimes we simply have to feel, and we have to feel that sense of being empty or devoid or being helpless or powerless. I wouldn't call it control, because I think it's a much deeper feeling than that.

Do you think it's easier for people if they have a strong religious faith, so that if something goes wrong, a terrible personal loss or setback, they've got something to rail against?

Well, as a psychotherapist that's not what I see. People who have terrible losses who have very deep religious beliefs . . . it's not that they rail against it, but it puts it in a context for them. So it's quite the opposite, in fact. They're not angry with their gods, they see this as 'this is what God offers them', as an explanation or a context for understanding these terrible disappointments.

So do you see God as some other form of therapy from your perspective, because you don't need him?

No, I don't. That's not to say that I don't think that people, the serious theologians around, for whom I've got a great respect, don't work the material that they've got in a therapeutic way – I think they do. They use God in a way to explore very interesting questions about the human experience and many of our dimensions. But no, I don't think of God as a form of therapy. Therapy does require active engagement. It isn't simply a balm. It's anything but a balm.

But I suppose a believer would say that God also requires active engagement?

Yes, I think for the believer God is a very significant relationship, but I'm not sure I'd call it therapy.

What about feminist attempts to remake God in their own image?

Those have been very interesting. A lot of American theologians, Lavinia Byrne here, have tried to look at God as a woman and look at the ways in which femininity has been presented and how we could represent it more fully. But when I look at the attempts of feminist theologians, or even liberation theologies, they seem to be much more akin to the political and philosophical conversations of our day. I'm happy to see the material they're taking on about equality, about integrity, about autonomy, connectedness, the complexity of who a woman is, about labour relations in liberation theology, but those don't seem to me to be profoundly religious questions. Those seem to me to be questions about how we survive, how we understand, how society is organised, and what we've inherited as a kind of social pattern and what we need to change.

Jung and Freud were divided over the role of religion. Freud thought it was something people should be freed from and that the desire for a personal god was 'infantile', whereas Jung once said about God that he didn't have to believe, he 'knew' he believed in a mystical subjective God. What do you think about those contrasting philosophies? I imagine you are nearer the Freudian one, but do they both make sense to you?

Yes. I think one of the extraordinary things about psychoanalysis is the capacity that one has to juggle contradictory ideas, which isn't to say that one is being a fake and not choosing, but at the same time as one understands the argument for atheism, which I embrace, I also understand the argument for a spiritual connection – it's just that I wouldn't describe it in the terms in which Jung would. I would describe it as what people create together, and their understanding of their relationship to others and their relationship to nature. I think that does reside in us and I think it is very, very moving.

It's interesting that you used the word 'atheism' . . . To be an atheist is to be an ultimately rational statement, isn't it? And yet you use the word 'spiritual'.

But it's also a statement of passion, it isn't simply a statement of rationality. Agnosticism would, for me, not work, because it would assume that there is something that I'm not really quite seeing that's called God. That doesn't work for me. No, I don't believe that there is a being that exists outside of us and yet inside of all of us, that's bigger than us – I don't. I do think humanity is a category that's much bigger than you or me and what we create together is profound and inspiring, but I don't call that God.

The word 'spiritual' is used very freely nowadays: People talk about all sorts of conflicting and complimentary New Age philosophies. Do you think they are, on balance, useful? This kind of broad amorphous feeling that there's more to life than the material?

Well, they clearly speak to people, and with the rapid acceleration of consumerism in Britain in the last thirty years and with the loss of a kind of political discourse, I can see why people are drawn to New Age religions or revitalising the religions they've come from. I think they do attempt to answer something. The question is whether or not it's the right answer, but I don't think we can say it's nonsense – it obviously speaks to people's needs to feel that they are part of something, that they are embracing something and they are embraced by something that is bigger than objects and has some dimension of transformation involved in it . . .

Where does your ongoing energy come from?

I do seem to have a fantastic amount of curiosity and interest in people's capacity to transform themselves. I think what you get from the consulting room is that you bear witness to people who feel broken down, are broken down, being able to find a meaningful purposeful way to go on, and that is absolutely magnificent to be part of. You're in the intimacy of that encounter with another. I grew up at a particular moment in history where I think my generation were very optimistic about what political changes it could bring about, but they haven't been brought about. But I think, in a way, I was marked by that optimism, the idea that we could change things, we could make pictures about how the world ought to be. And I suppose as I've got older I think you have to listen to a lot of other people all the time – you can't simply impose the ideas that you had, and people have very, very good ideas. But where my optimism comes from I'm not entirely sure. I'm also deeply pessimistic. I think those two things are not quite balanced, but there is a part of me that has a lot of despair, and I don't actually think you can have optimism that's devoid of despair because it would be too synthetic. There is optimism knowing that we have to deal with what you call 'evil' but what I might call 'cruelty' or 'distortions' or 'inhumanity' – I think we have to deal with that. We've just come out of a century of industrialised killing. We can't be optimistic unless we take that on board and try to understand the roots of that and how we're capable, both as individuals and collectively, to enact these horrors upon each other.

Are there moments in your life when you have a sense of what one might call transcendence?

I think there are a lot of different forms of transcendence. It might just be looking at a rose in Queen Mary's Rose Garden and smelling it, or it might be writing a sentence that says more than I hoped it could possibly say, or having a very good conversation or cooking a very good meal. So I don't know if I've got the right vocabulary when I say 'transcendence', but it's something about a moment being more than itself and having an aesthetic that's also around it, which has within it a very moving dimension. Does that do it? I don't know.

(2001 conversation)

David Owen

Created a life peer in 1992, Lord Owen was born in Plymouth in 1938 and studied medicine at Cambridge and St Thomas's Hospital, London. He was MP for Plymouth from 1966 to 1992, Minister for the Navy, Minister of Health and Foreign Secretary, and helped found the SDP, becoming its leader from 1983. From 1992 to 1995 he was European Union Co-Chairman of the International Conference on the Former Yugoslavia.

I can't think of any better place to start than in your grandfather's study in Wales. Tell me about that room, about him.

The room was interesting in that one whole, rather long side was completely composed of the Bible in Braille. He was blind, and those were the days when books were difficult to do, and the whole of that wall was the Bible. And he would pick up this particular section, and he'd pass his hands just lightly over the paper and pick up the dots, and would read the Bible without any interruption at all. A completely constant flow. And it was a wonderful experience. We used to play a game: I would come into the room on all fours and try to pretend I wasn't there. And then suddenly he'd lift a slipper off his foot and throw it at me, and invariably hit me!

But he was a remarkable man – a clergyman in the Church of Wales. He started as a Methodist and then, when the Church was disestablished, he felt much happier in the Church in Wales and went on to get a doctorate of divinity. He was a very distinguished figure, really, in the Welsh church. He was a canon, but he never became a bishop. It was difficult for him to move parishes, and he stayed in one parish in south Glamorgan.

You stayed with him during the war when your father was away. What effect did that have on you?

He taught me to read, and I used to go to the village school. I learned Welsh at that stage. But I think he taught me much more. He taught me about life, to wonder at nature. He taught me self-discipline, little small things. Every time he got out of bed he would fold his pyjamas. He was immensely careful. He was no saint, but he was a good man.

He preached the Christianity of love. For him, Christianity was all about love and nothing shifted or changed. There are words which sum up his view, and I actually think it might be better to give it to you from the 1929 Book of Common Prayer: it says, 'The Lord our God is one Lord: and thou shalt love the Lord thy God with all thy heart, and with all thy soul, and with all thy mind, and with all thy strength: this is the first commandment. And the second is like, namely this: thou shalt love thy neighbour as thyself. There is none other commandment greater than these. On these two commandments hang all the law and the prophets.' And for me, that is religion. I realise that everybody else will have different views. And I realise that it is necessary to have a church, and it's necessary to have a doctrine of faith and belief. But I think we must be tolerant of each other, and that was the doctrine he preached to me. Everything rested on love – the love of God – and if you could accept that, then don't get yourself too fussed about other things.

Sadly, he died when I was only thirteen. I wish he'd lived longer. But when I was starting to question things, he'd always come back to, 'Just focus on one thing: the love of God and the love of your fellow men.'

On the other side of your family, your paternal great-grandfather was a Congregationalist minister, and he spent some time hot-gospelling in the States. The pulpit is surely in your blood. Weren't you intensely religious as a young man?

Intensely? Probably, yes. It's never been out of my life, and it's there. I don't talk about it, or I usen't to talk about it when I was a politician, because I felt that it was not right to intrude in what was basically a secular activity. But it's there. I'm not a very good believer in the sense of taking a lot of what is preached by the Church of England or the Church in Wales literally. But that doesn't trouble me. I hope it doesn't trouble the priests who I take communion with. I'm not a tremendous attender of church, but when I can, my wife and I go.

It was unusual you carried your faith through your teens and to Cambridge, because that's the time when people frequently rebel. In your autobiography, Time to Declare, *you suggest that at times you were close to becoming a religious fanatic. What form did that take?*

I'm surprised I used the word 'fanatic'. I've never been really fanatical on anything. At that time in Cambridge, the clergyman I most admired was Mervyn Stockwood, who was your classic turbulent priest. He was agin the establishment and agin the government of the day. I arrived at Cambridge and the Suez Crisis was still on, and then the Soviet Union invaded Hungary. So it was a very emotional time, and you had a clergyman who took a very strong view. His church was packed out. People queued to go into Great St Mary's in those days. So it was easier to be very committed because it was so relevant to what was being preached . . .

And you were drawn to Christianity as a radical moral force within society.

Yes. I thought Christian socialism was a natural partner. I don't think I've ever thought that you can't have any other political belief. I'm very catholic – with a small 'c' – about religion, and indeed, a lot of things. I believe in diversity. I don't believe there is a single path. I think it's more complicated than that. You must be tolerant . . . everybody has a different, individual way of expressing their faith or non-faith.

You were trained as a natural scientist, and I wonder if that told you that the old simplicities of faith simply couldn't be true.

I didn't find so. I was very interested in Teilhard de Chardin, for instance, when I was reading for a natural science degree. He was a scientist himself and he managed to square his scientific views with his religious faith . . . If you wish to be literal and you want to believe in the virgin birth in its fullest sense, that's fine. I can understand why people want to do that. I understand why a religion has built up around the virgin birth and the immaculate conception. It's all part of the need for people to have myth in their life, miracles in their life; to believe things, to not always have to *know* everything. These are all varied factors. But for me – perhaps helped by my grandfather – it wasn't something that I have to get terribly fussed about. I can hear him now: he would just say, 'Don't worry about this.' If it comes to you, you believe in the virgin birth, if you satisfy yourself – as I think he did, probably, I don't really know; his attitude would be, 'That doesn't matter. Focus on what's important.' What religion gives you is some power outside yourself to be better than you are and to understand the power of love.

Before medical school at St Thomas's in London, you went on a trip to Afghanistan, India and Iran, and you've described this as a great spiritual experience in your life. What happened?

I experienced a number of great religions, which I hadn't – in a rather sheltered life in the West Country and even at Cambridge –

really at that stage experienced. I drove through the Muslim countries of Turkey and Iran, and then actually lived with the tribesmen in Afghanistan and shared their tent, shared their meals. And you saw all the different aspects of the Muslim faith, really, in that short journey. And then later I went to India and saw the Hindu faith; and then in both Afghanistan, Pakistan and India, you saw the Buddhist faith. So you saw three great religions. After that, quite honestly, it was not possible to believe that what I'd learned from my grandfather in Wales was universal and had to be adopted by everybody. It seemed to me utterly crazy. So I became an ecumenicalist, and I have remained one . . .

. . . You chose to be a doctor. You could heal the sick. I wonder what makes a person who can do obvious good, like that take the primrose path into politics and power? Is it a version of the temptation of Christ?

I can only reflect the times, in the early 1960s. St Thomas's Hospital looks rather prosperous, opposite the House of Commons, but actually behind it in those days – and even now – was some very bad housing and some poor conditions, and I think I grew more and more to believe, as I was doing my medical studies, that the answer to a lot of ill health was not a new pill. It was actually in better housing and better social conditions and better education. I know people find it very difficult to believe, but I almost went into politics by accident, and certainly very few people have entered the House of Commons with less involvement with a political party and things. Maybe that's been my political life. It's always been independent, and one of the reasons it's been independent is actually that I was always very happy to go back to medicine. It was never any problem. I had a very marginal seat, so I actually faced the reality almost every election that I might well be looking for a job, and undoubtedly I would have gone back to medicine.

At thirty-eight you were famously the youngest Foreign Secretary since Sir Anthony Eden, and then you became disillusioned with the Labour Party, broke away to form the SDP with Shirley Williams and William Rogers. Now, at that time and subsequently, you attracted an awful lot of flack, personal abuse. A lot of people felt you'd betrayed them. I don't want to talk about the politics of that, but I wonder if there was any religious dimension to your survival at those bad times.

I don't think so, really. I think the love of my family mattered a great deal, and the love of quite a number of people in politics who came with me down that journey . . .

During all this time, you were enduring something far more painful, which was the long illness, from leukaemia, of one of your children. And you and your wife, Deborah Owen, the literary agent, had to sit by his bed in Great Ormond Street, afflicted with the knowledge that he could die. I'm wondering at that time if you ever instructed – and I use that word rather than 'asked' – God to help your son. You said you put your faith in doctors. Did you put any faith in the God of your grandfather?

Oh yes, definitely. But I think I'd lived enough of life, seeing so much death in medicine, seeing – unfortunately – rather a lot of death in Africa as Foreign Secretary, before I dealt with Yugoslavia, to know that people die and there is no reason to it, and that part of faith is being able to live through that. Now we were all fortunate in that he survived and is a healthy young man with his own career in front of him and has done wonderfully well. But I am to this day eternally grateful to the doctors of Great Ormond Street for what they did, and I have no doubt that I was sustained through that personally by faith. It was a very important factor. We may have been very individualistic and different, and didn't have all the trappings of the organised faith, but it was powerful for me.

When you write about this episode in your book – very movingly – it's interesting that you emphasise what I can only describe as the power of love, and how you would will *him to get better.*

He willed himself to get better. That's more important. We did will him, and many friends and many people not terribly well known to us prayed for him, and it's a very humbling thing when you realise that is happening around the world for many, many different people. But what was more important about him was his courage, and the way he willed himself to get better. He fought that illness. Now I believe in this, and I always tell people – people with cancer – they may have been given some very bad news and very bad prognosis. And I say to them, 'Never underestimate the capacity of the human body to recover, and never underestimate the capacity of the human will to make the body recover.' And I believe that. Now that strength, I think, comes from a force outside of yourself. I will call it God, but others don't have to believe in God. They may call it by another name. And I believe in that power that we don't understand.

And the possibility of the miraculous?

I think it does exist, yes. I don't know. There are lots of different miracles through history. Some seem more genuine than others. But it's not too big a leap of faith for me to believe there are miracles, and that some of those miracles owe their power to something which is not in oneself . . .

Considering humanity and considering harm takes us inevitably into the valley of the shadow, and I mean Bosnia. Your role as mediator in the Yugoslav civil war – you were appointed in 1992 – exposed you to what you've called 'savage, shameful acts'. And the language that you have used to describe that period: you talk about 'a sewer, a cesspit' – it's very, very powerful. In retrospect, do you use words like 'evil' to describe what happened there?

Oh yes. I believe in evil. I think that's quite an important part of religion, but I definitely believe in evil, and I think that one of the tasks of the politician is to delineate evil and recognise evil, and stand up to evil . . . You are affected by your experience, but I don't think it had any particular . . . it didn't question my faith in God or religion. There were many different conflicting religions, which was one of the factors behind it. It didn't really change my belief that politicians have to dirty their hands on behalf of other people. Sometimes governments have to ask somebody to do it for them, and in this case a negotiator. I think it was a time, if you like, of payback for me. I'd had a pretty charmed political life in many respects. I'd held high office, way beyond what I could have expected, and I think you have an opportunity to put something back. So nobody can say, 'This was a bloody awful task.' When I was asked to do it by the European Union, it was made absolutely clear to me that it was a lousy job. Lord Carrington had just given it up. The prospects of any success were not very high, but nevertheless it had to be done and I think it was right to do it.

. . . We can just hope to make the world, slowly, bit by bit, inch by inch, a better place, and deal with some of the most terrible things that happen. I certainly think that genocide is an evil that has to be dealt with by force. We can argue about how much genocide there was in Yugoslavia. The court is deciding that there was some genocide. But I've lived with this. After all, I spent two and a half years as Foreign Secretary negotiating in the midst of guerrilla war in Rhodesia, which is now Zimbabwe. One hoped that that would solve the problem of Zimbabwe. Now it's back there. I suppose as you get older you learn that there is a cycle to these events, but there is also a cycle to peace. I remember negotiating over Namibia in 1978, down in South Africa: and the UN resolution that came out of that negotiation eventually, twelve years later, was the basis for Namibia coming to independence. So you have to learn as a politician, particularly in foreign and international affairs, that some of the things you do may only really show benefit over quite a long time. You have to have faith in that. You have to be patient . . .

(2002 conversation)

Philip Pullman

Philip Pullman became the first 'children's' author to win the Whitbread Book of the Year with *The Amber Spyglass* (the third volume in the trilogy *His Dark Materials*) in 2001. He has won many other awards for his work, including the Carnegie Medal. Born in 1946, he became a teacher before devoting himself to writing full time.

What's it like to become a cult?

Well, I could tell you if I knew that I *was* the centre of a cult. I don't think it is a cult. Cult implies, doesn't it, a small band of loyal and intensely fanatical followers? I hope that my readers are not that small in number and are not intensely fanatical about it. I like to feel that I've got a wider readership with this book than I've had with any other, and I think that's true. Letters that I get from young children, from teenagers and from adults as well, sort of bear this out. So if it's a cult, it's a funny sort of one.

We should explain to those who don't know: you used the word 'book' but what we're actually talking about is a trilogy, with the overall title of His Dark Materials. *It's been reviewed all over the world, there are reading groups devoted to it, teachers teach it. It's been denounced by the* Catholic Herald, *and adults puzzle over your meanings. Do you think such a response to this trilogy proves that, for people of all ages, the struggle between good and evil is the ultimate story?*

I wouldn't put it quite like that, I'd say the struggle between meaning and insignificance. What I mean is, we are born into the world without any clear signposts as to why we came here and where we are going. And yet, in the hearts of most of us – I daresay there are some people who don't feel this, but in the hearts of many, many people – there is a longing for significance, for meaning, for answers to the question, 'Why? What's it all about? Why are we here? What have we got to do?' and so on. 'What happens when we die?' and so on.

  In writing this book, I was not trying to give answers to these questions, but to give expression to the questions. I think I could put it like that. Clearly this resonates with a lot of people. The central story, not to be too detailed about it, concerns the same story as is told in the third chapter of the book of Genesis: the loss of innocence. Growing up, in other words. Growing up and discovering a sense of self, a sense of right and wrong, and a sense of sexuality, too – a growing awareness of one's own body and its effects on other people. This is a very simple story. It's been told a thousand times in different forms, and here I am, telling it again. But it is a central story to all of us. We all grow up. We all get older. We all have been children.

And we all want to understand, as you said, the meaning of the universe.

Children do, especially. Young readers are passionate about this. When we grow up, we're sort of overtaken by the pressures of daily life, the needs to earn a living, to keep your job, to try and keep your head in all the pressures of life, and so on. And we forget, or we don't have the chance, to think through these big problems. We sort of put them on the back burner – 'Oh, I'll take care of that when I'm older, later on.'

But for children who don't have that sort of pressure – for young teenagers especially, who are just beginning to move out of childhood and become aware of such things as art, music, poetry, philosophy, the great questions of life, science, the excitement of that, and questions of justice and right and wrong in the world, and politics – this is a tremendously exciting time in life. So it's natural that a book that does perhaps put these questions in a different way should find a resonance with people who are going through that experience . . .

Let's go back to your own view of God and how it was formed and, perhaps, how you ditched it. You were brought up by your grandfather, who was a clergyman . . .

I spent a lot of my childhood in the household of my grandfather – my mother's father. My father died when I was seven. We moved about a lot in my childhood. My grandfather was the rector of a parish in Norfolk. His rectory was always the sort of still centre of that world in which I was wandering about, and it was always a great joy to go to Grandpa's house and spend the holidays there – and go to church and listen to him preach, and listen to his stories, and play with all the bits and pieces he had lying around the house.

He, of course, was a Victorian. He was born in 1890 and grew up with all the certainties and all the rock-hard moral convictions of that age. He was a very kindly man, but he was also – how can I put it? – not a subtle man. And although he was full of Christian compassion, I think there were areas where he couldn't quite join the modern world. He was certain, for example, of the value of capital punishment. Now I mentioned this because he was a prison chaplain, and it was part of his duties to attend executions in Norwich Prison, which caused him to suffer greatly, of course. It was his job to spend the last hour of the condemned man's life with him, and go to the scaffold with him. This was a very, very difficult thing for him to do, but I don't recall him ever saying that capital punishment was a bad thing.

So was the God you heard him preach about from his pulpit a vengeful God?

No, no. The God was a very kind one. I remember very vividly a story he told about a friend of his. Grandpa came from a large farming Devonshire family. And a friend of his from the village – a chap called Fred Austin – went off to the First World War, as Grandpa did. And he had a little daughter, and he was away at the front in France for a couple of years – or a long time, anyway. When he came back home, his little daughter didn't recognise this big, fierce man who came home, and she was frightened. She ran away. But Grandpa told me that Fred Austin was wonderful to see as he gently, over the next few days, coaxed her, and finally she came to accept that he was gentle and kind and loving. Now Grandpa used this as a parable of what God is like. 'God is like Fred Austin. First we flee from him, and then gradually we see how loving he is, and how kind he is.'

That story resonated for me for all sorts of reasons, not least because it's paralleled almost exactly in the *Iliad,* when Hector, on the walls of Troy, turns to take his little son from the arms of his nurse, and the son is frightened at the father's great war helmet with its nodding plume, and he cries and he turns away. When I was telling the story of the *Iliad* to the children I used to teach, I was thinking of Fred Austin. So these stories resonate, illustrate and illuminate each other, down through the ages, and they come to life in the most vivid and homely little details. But that was my grandfather's view of God, as a kindly God, not a vengeful one.

It's very interesting to me that your whole experience of the Church, then, when you were young, was benign, and the teachings of your grandfather were clearly good – leaving capital punishment out of it. Why did you turn away with such vehemence? In the last volume of the trilogy especially, God is the 'Authority', and the Church, the 'Magisterium', is just a force for evil. Why are you so vehemently anti organised religion?

Simply from looking at history. A large proportion of what the Christian Church has done has been intolerant, cruel, fanatical, whichever part of the spectrum you look at, whether it's the Inquisition with the Catholics burning the heretics, or whether it's the other end of the spectrum – the Puritans in New England, burning the witches or hanging the witches, rather. Wherever you look you see intolerance, cruelty, fanaticism, narrow-mindedness. It's an ugly, ugly spectacle.

Well, historically there's no gainsaying that, but when I finished The Amber Spyglass *one of the many things I thought was, Philip Pullman obviously hates the Church, but all the clerics I meet are decent, bearded chaps in the half-empty churches, doing good works and bringing comfort to pensioners. They're not burning witches.*

Not any more. They wouldn't get away with it now.

But they wouldn't want to.

No, not the nice gentle ones who have half-empty churches. But the ones who have churches that are full – the evangelicals, the fundamentalists – are full of hell-fire and damnation and fury and vengeance on anyone who disagrees with them. To step outside of the Christian religion, aren't there parts of the world now where you can be treated with extraordinary cruelty for speaking out against the local religion?

In all the reviews and articles about this trilogy, the name C.S. Lewis tends to crop up. You're quite rude about him.

He was, of course, a popular theologian, a popular apologist for Christianity, and his books on religion had a huge circulation in the 1930s and 1940s, particularly during the war when he was also a broadcaster. He wrote the seven Narnia books at great speed, with a sort of white-hot emotional pressure. Now the religion which he is depicting in the Narnia books is, to me, one of the ugliest manifestations of Christianity we've ever seen. For example, at the climax of the whole story, when the children who've gone through all these great adventures are entering the stable which represents salvation, one of them is shut out. And this is the girl, Susan, because, as the boy Peter says rather primly, 'My sister is no longer a friend to Narnia.' And one of the other children says, 'Yes. Susan is also far too keen on growing up. She's interested in nothing but nylons and lipstick and so on.' So what this implies is the normal course of development of an adolescent child – nylons and lipstick are, of course, emblematic of an interest in your own body and the way it affects other people's bodies, your growing awareness of your own sexuality and so on. This is enough to damn her in perpetuity.

Aren't you being a bit unfair – because they were written quite some time ago, a different age?

But they're still in print. They're hailed as great Christian works. It's a horrific view. And at the very end of the book, the very end of the last battle, what happens? All these children who have presumably grown up and learned things through all these adventures and taken, as I would put it, the first steps on the road to becoming wise and useful citizens, what happens to them? They're all killed in a railway accident. 'The term is over,' says Aslan, 'the holidays have begun.' So the world is such a corrupt and foul place that his children have to be taken out of it. Again, this seems to be a betrayal. It's a betrayal of life. It's a negation of life. It's a vote for death instead of life. It's a vote for the unreal instead of the real.

But at the end of The Last Battle, *the depiction of the other world reminded me of some of your descriptions of physical beauty, and if it's heaven for C.S. Lewis, is that so different from your dead becoming a part of the universe in the wonderful way you describe?*

Very different. Because I insist that this world is here, now, and that we are in it. And he says, no, we're not. It's elsewhere, and we have to die before we get there . . .

In the trilogy, as well as retelling Genesis, you are invoking Paradise Lost *– a tremendously important influence which gave the overall title,* His Dark Materials. *Your thesis is that when the rebel angel, Satan, lost the war in heaven and was plunged down into the pit with his fellow rebels, essentially, the wrong side won.*

Now, I have to go back a little bit to explain what I mean by this. Underneath the surface of this story there is . . . I suppose you could call it a creation myth, just as underlying the surface story of *Paradise Lost* there is the myth of the creation as we know it from the Bible and from Christian tradition. Satan rebelled through pride and was cast into hell, and then, out of vengeance, concocted a plan to tempt the new human beings that God had created and so lead them out of Paradise: that's the story that underlies *Paradise Lost*. Now, underlying my story there is another myth, a similar myth. The figure whom I call the Authority, the Father, God, was not the creator. We don't know who the creator was. Maybe there was no creator. Maybe everything just was. He was the first angel, and in his pride he declared to the other creatures, the other angels around him, that he had created them. So it was all a lie from the beginning: there was no creator. He set himself up over the rest of them. Against him there rebelled a number of angels, including the figure called Wisdom – Sophia . . . This figure of Wisdom is the one who originally helped human beings to become free – in other words, did what Milton portrays Satan as doing in the Garden of Eden: tempted them by telling them about good and evil. In my story, the Sophia, the figure of Wisdom, comes to human beings at a certain stage in their evolution and helps them to realise who they are, to break free of the pettiness of childhood, of the ignorance which is innocence, and take the first steps towards becoming wise, towards wisdom. If you want to contrast these two things, innocence is not wise, and wisdom cannot be innocent.

It's as if you have such a passionate and strong sense of the divine, but you dislike divinity.

That's an interesting proposition. I've never had it put it quite like that. 'A sense of the divine' I'm not sure about. One of the elements in my trilogy is something called Dust. Dust is a mysterious force which seems to settle on people when they're grown up, and it frightens, it terrifies, the agents of the Church, because it seems to them in some way equivalent to original sin, or to derive from original sin, or to bring original sin with it, or something like that. They're not sure. As I depict Dust – which Lyra, my heroine, comes to realise is a force for good and which she must find out more about – it seems to be both a product of and a generating force for human wisdom; for goodness; for curiosity about things; for human affection; for all the things that we would be glad to have as part of our grown-up personalities.

We are not just the product of Dust. We ourselves partly generate Dust, so we are both in it and of it and we give birth to it. This seems to me, if one wanted to find a metaphor for a god in whom I could believe, rather better than saying that there is someone who created you and you are his subject and his creature, and you owe obedience and a dutiful love to him, and you will be blessed or damned after you die, as he thinks fit – which is, of course, totally incredible. I like my metaphor of Dust. I like the fact that we are, in some sense, contributing to this, as well as being part of it and born of it, and will rejoin it, and so on. So this picture of Dust is, I suppose, the nearest I will get, or the nearest I have got, to a sense of the divine. It's present in poetry, too. Wordsworth: 'Something far more deeply interfused . . .' and all that sort of stuff.

It's a very important part of your work that you believe in original goodness, not original sin.

Yes. I don't like the idea of original sin because it seems to me too closely bound up with our attempts to become knowledgeable, to become wise. It's the tree of the knowledge of good and evil, eating that tree, which led to our sinfulness, and I don't find that idea at all attractive. Goodness and sinfulness, goodness and evil, or whatever, are both bound up in us in every stage of our lives. But I cannot see the human attempts to become wise, to know more, to become more informed about the world, as being anything but good. How could they be anything but good?

The soul is a key idea in your trilogy. Tell me a little bit about how you visualise it.

When we first meet the main character of the book, Lyra, in the first sentence of the first book, we meet her in the company of her daemon – I spell it like that in order to distinguish it obviously from demons and devils. 'Lyra and her daemon' are the first four words of the book, and we soon become aware that everybody in this world – which is so like ours but so different in many ways – everybody has a daemon. And this daemon seems to function – and I don't explain it, I let it emerge as the story develops – this daemon is a part of their personality, it seems to be part of them. A lot of questions I got were, 'Is the daemon a soul?' 'Is this what you mean by the soul?' And I would say, 'Wait and see what happens.' Because, of course, as Lyra discovers in the third part of the book, she can think about her body and she can think about her daemon. Now there must be a third part of her to be doing the thinking, and this is the part I call the ghost. I don't use the word 'soul', I think, anywhere in the book. I talk about body, daemon and ghost. In this underlying myth of mine – this creation myth – I discovered for myself where these three elements came from, and I'll probably explain it in a further book in the future.

The ghost is the part that survives death, but survives it only to find itself in a sort of concentration camp which is the world of the dead, which was set up by the Authority – my God figure – in order to punish human beings, many, many years ago, for their first disobedience. One of the things that Lyra and Will do in the world of the dead is to discover how to liberate the ghosts of all those who have died. They do this, and the liberation takes the form of being released once more, to dissolve as their bodies and their daemons have dissolved into the physical world. This is the picture I have provided of the soul, although I don't call it the soul. The daemon is part of the soul, as well. There's body, daemon and ghost. These are the three parts of us.

The daemon takes the shape of an animal, of the opposite gender to the character, who changes shape until the child is adult. Why did you come up with that idea, that it becomes fixed in adulthood?

When I first wrote *Northern Lights* [the first book in the trilogy] and I discovered that Lyra had a daemon and that her daemon could change shape, I wrote the first chapter and there were adults in the story as well, of course, and their daemons changed shape as well. They all had an animal daemon, and from time to time they changed shape, according to the mood of the character, or whatever. Then I stopped and thought, 'What is this actually saying? What is this telling the reader? What is this providing a picture of?' And the answer came: 'Well, nothing very much. It's just a picturesque detail,' which I could see would quickly become annoying unless I related it in some way to the theme of the whole story, which was growing up – the difference between children and grown ups. I was walking about, trying to find the answer to this, and, of course, it occurred to me after not too great a time of walking up and down. But I can still remember the moment and the place in the garden where this occurred to me. It was such an exciting moment. Children's daemons change, and then they stop changing when they become adult. In this, I found a richness of possibilities that I was still exploring at the very end of the trilogy. It seemed to me so pregnant with all kinds of meanings and truths about the way we live, and the way we grow up, and the way we understand each other, and the way we stop changing. We lose the plasticity, the infinite potentiality of childhood, but we gain something by losing that. We gain strength and certainty. We know more about who we are.

Do you believe in any form of life after death?

I believe pretty well what I've described in the third book, in *The Amber Spyglass*. I believe in something like what happens in the world of the dead. Lyra is a story-teller. She's a liar, she's a fabulist. She discovers that the harpies who guard the world of the dead are not satisfied by the sort of stories she's been telling them to that point. 'Liar!' they call her. 'Liar!' which resonates with her name, Lyra. But the ghosts of the children beg her to tell them again about the world. 'Remind us what it was like. Tell us about the sunshine, the real world.' So she does. She tells them about the fun she had when she was back in her home city, and playing on the river bank, and all that sort of stuff. As she tells this story, and uses all her craft and all her command of words to summon up a picture of the real world, she suddenly becomes aware that the harpies are listening. This is what they have wanted to hear all these years. They want to hear the real stories, people's true stories. And so the way out of the world of the dead is first to make sure you have lived enough to experience the world. If you spend your whole life playing video games and watching the telly – no good. They won't be satisfied with that. This is why you've got to live, you see, but then be able to tell your story to the harpies who guard the world of the dead, and that will free you to join the world again and be, as it were, recycled.

They go out into the world, and they become atoms. They just disperse. And you use the metaphor of bubbles in a champagne glass.

This, for them at that point, is the most sweet and desirable end they could possibly imagine, and they come to it with utter joy.

Is that how you visualise your own end?

I would like to. I think I probably do. But I'm not there yet.

You've said in interviews, 'This is all there is, this life on earth, this experience,' and that 'We have to build the republic of heaven here.' Do you have enough faith that we, humankind, can do that?

It's pretty finely balanced. When you look at the news sometimes, you despair. But then you look at the achievements of the human race and you feel optimistic again. It swings this way and that. I think I'm 51 per cent optimistic. I think I have to be. This is another odd little thing. It isn't just a matter of temperament. It's a moral duty, isn't it, to be optimistic? 'Faith, hope and charity, abide these three . . . the greatest of them is charity.' I agree with that. But hope is there as well. We have a duty to be optimistic about this. It helps. It actually works if you believe that 51 per cent is good and 49 per cent is not.

Given where you began – given your grandfather's teaching, which was totally benign – you can't see any way in which you would be drawn back?

Well, who can tell what one will be driven to on one's deathbed? But I like the attitude of whoever it was, this life-long atheist, who said, 'God will forgive me. It's his job.' And I agree: *c'est son métier.* So I think if there is a god, it is his job to forgive me for having blasphemed against him for all these years.

(2001 conversation)

Clare Short

The Rt Hon. Clare Short has been MP (Labour) for Birmingham Ladywood since 1983, and Secretary of State for International Development from 1997 until her resignation in 2003. She was Director of All Faiths for One Race, Birmingham, from 1976 to 1978, and has published three books, including a handbook of immigration law.

If your grandchildren were to ask you one day, 'What is God?' what would you say?

I would say God is the encapsulation of everything that is good – and humanity turned that into an old man with a beard because that was the only way they could imagine it. It's not a person, but it is a beautiful and very important thing.

Would you have said the same when you were twelve?

No. I did my catechism: 'Who made you? God made you. Why did God make you?' There must be something there. I was brought up very thoroughly as a Catholic in a way that I really liked and took very seriously, and I think I thought God was quite a stern God who said what was right and wrong and you had to do it or be damned. I used to go to sleep at night when I was seven, praying – this is a Catholic tradition – for the last soul in purgatory, because these are the neglected ones. And I used to imagine the last one overtaking the next to last one and my prayers having to be transferred to the new last one. So when I was twelve I went with all the literal and old-fashioned ideas of a rather strict judgmental God.

Did that make for a universe which was actually fearful?

No. I always loved the world. It's just that as I got to be fourteen, fifteen, sixteen, it didn't stack up. The ideas I'd been taught, that I'd taken so seriously about what was right and what was wrong, increasingly didn't chime. Although I came from the old-fashioned strict Catholicism I was never really scared of God. I always quite liked him.

Was that part of your parents' teaching, because you come from a very large and devout Catholic family and religion played a large part in your family life?

Yes. My mother still lives with me in Birmingham and she's a very dedicated Catholic, though of a sort of liberation theology type. She would say of her children – there's seven of us – that she slightly regrets that the version of Catholicism we got wasn't the love-driven one, it was the rules one. She thinks that most of us were lost to it by that. My father, on the other hand, who is dead but who was also a devout practising Catholic . . . for him it was very much part of his identity as an Irishman, a thing that the British had tried to beat out of the Irish historically – you know, the penal times and so on – so he was much more rational about religion and more critical, less emotional about his Catholicism. So already, within the model we had there were different kinds of versions and nuances, but it was very Catholic.

And presumably for both your parents, although coming at it from those different angles, the idea of God overlapped with politics . . . a just God?

Oh, absolutely. Religion is all about what is right and what is wrong, both for the world order and for your own life, and so is politics. Being involved in politics is to stand up for what is right, so the two were just part and parcel of the same quest. In the way I grew up it would be hard to think (and I know this sounds terrible) that a Tory could be a Christian. I know better now, and it wasn't that I was ever taught to criticise others – but it was the values we had, and clearly we had to be right. We knew people like us were often not victorious, when you look at history, but you have to stand up for what's right no matter how long it takes. That was just part of the politics and part of the religion.

So how come you made this shift away from religion and more towards politics, given they'd been so much entangled?

I remember when I was fourteen or fifteen, this question of contraception . . . the thing is the Pope says you can't use contraception and this is quite ridiculous, of course. Therefore he's wrong and therefore . . . And then, of course, Catholicism pays the price of its clarity because if the Pope's wrong then he might be wrong about something else . . . So increasingly I didn't believe in the teachings of the Church, thought they were wrong about some things, began to doubt the existence of a personal God. I've never disrespected religion or indeed the idea of a god, but a lot of the details of the teaching. My mum didn't like this much and found a sort of trendy American visitor priest and sent me off, and we had a nice chat and I sort of went back a bit, but it was going from me, and by the time I was seventeen . . . My mum then said, 'You must go to Mass when you're at home or you'll give a bad example to the little ones.' And I said, 'Yes, of course.' And once I'd left home and went to university I went to one Catholic thing, and then I didn't go – and it wasn't like 'I've escaped these rules', it's 'I don't believe in it and I respect it so much I'm not going to do it hypocritically.'

It's very interesting, in the kind of constituency I represent, because it's very mixed and multi-ethnic; I have the centre of Birmingham, so I have all the great world religions there and I get invited to various celebrations. I go and I'm very moved by it – by the religious. I think it is wonderful and important that there are spaces in local churches where the questions of what is right and what is wrong are reflected upon, and great beautiful texts are read that talk about the most profound moral and human questions. I love and honour religion, and I have my own sort of version: like the idea of God is the encapsulation of goodness, and the wish to honour God is the wish to honour the quest after goodness, which is a wholly fine thing. And immortality is not that we're going to be in heaven and live, but that every single human being that's ever lived will leave traces behind them on this earth for good or ill, and that's a form of immortality. Of course, every one of us that has ever loved anybody knows they will be alive in us until we die, and that's another form of immortality.

And, for example, the Christian teaching of sin – that you have to try to be good but won't always succeed, that we will do wrong sometimes, that we can be forgiven but we have to be truly sorry, but you can be forgiven and try again, you're not written off – that's very important and right. So I go in and out of these churches and I have these deep experiences and I love all that space, but I don't believe in a personal god and I haven't got my own one. Sometimes I feel a bit lonely and I go with my mum to the church that I was baptised in, my parents were married in. It's just there on the edge of my constituency; I made my first communion and my confirmation there and I love it, and I think sometimes that perhaps I could have my funeral there.

I'm an ethnic Catholic, profoundly shaped by my Catholic upbringing.

My politics are a continuation of that quest, and so in that sense I'm still one of those old-fashioned Labour people – the Labour party is my church. I'm in it because I want to work for the decent moral order in our country and in the world . . . it's a religion. It's not an alternative religion. I know this doesn't seem to fit with modern politics, but that's me.

A lot of people reject the Church, as indeed you did and I did as a teenager, because you think so many bad things have been done in the name of religion, whether it's making women have lots of babies or worse . . .

The Catholic Church and Franco, for example . . .

Exactly. But lots of awful things are also done in the name of socialism. Was that a problem for you?

I hate awful things being done to anyone, but I've never been tempted by any of them. Those ones were never socialism. If I'd lived in the Soviet Union I would have been in a gulag – I've said it in committees in the House of Commons. My socialism is ethical. It never was an Economic System Socialism – it's an ethic that says every single human being is of equal moral value, and we have to try and organise the world to recognise that and give everyone equal moral space to be valued to enable them to live a full life.

So it's not that different from the kind of ethical Christianity which stood up to communism in Eastern Europe and fascism in South America?

Some Christians have been very principled and fine people and some have been monsters. My father used to say, when I was starting to have my doubts, he said, 'Remember, Clare, Christianity was the religion of the slaves. It spread through the Roman Empire among the slaves because it said everyone is equal in the sight of God.' That's a very important argument . . .

Would it be true to say that, having removed yourself from the Catholicism of your parents, by moving to socialism what you're actually doing all the time in your life is expressing a belief in the perfectibility of humankind?

'Perfectibility' sounds as though we're in a sort of lost condition and we can improve ourselves. I think human beings are intrinsically incredibly beautiful. They're capable of being damaged. They're capable of great and heroic and beautiful things and they're capable of being crass and mean and unjust and cruel, and I think human life is about the journey of trying to be the better side of what we are. You'll never be perfect, but you have to keep struggling with yourself and trying to work for the world, which maximises that beautiful goodness, knowing that it will never always be perfect, that we have to have a way of accommodating our own personal inadequacy and other people's and our incapacity to be what we are at our most beautiful. So that isn't quite perfectibility, but it's that struggle between good and evil – in how we organise the world and how we live our own lives and how we relate to other human beings.

But when you talk about the struggle between good and evil, for you that's in humankind, it's not 'out there'?

Yes, it's *in* us. I think we are intrinsically fine and lovely creatures, but we are capable of evil and if we treat any one of us with great cruelty it tends to make people become bad. One of the things I've learned is that most cruelty and evil comes from weak and damaged people. It doesn't therefore mean that you don't blame them, but you can see. You go into Winson Green Prison in the middle of my constituency and some of those people have done really bad things, but ever such a lot of them are messed up and not educated and mentally damaged, so there's a dilemma. Hate the sin and not the sinner. Don't forgive anything that's evil, because it doesn't matter how damaged you are, part of being a human being is that you have to take moral responsibility for yourself. But understand that it's not fair, that we all start from different places, that some people are very damaged and hurt, and if they've had lots of ugliness and cruelty they haven't learned their full moral capability. These are big questions, but they're in politics all the time.

So you can believe in wickedness but at the same time preach what Christ preached, which is the possibility of redemption?

That is the human condition. We can be wicked. Some people are very wicked. They can be forgiven. They have to be sorry, really profoundly and truly sorry. This is Christian teaching, but it's now completely incorporated in my world view. I think it's profoundly right. It's, of course, in all the other great world religions. On these deep moral questions of human life, of course, they agree.

To that extent you wouldn't put the religion of your childhood as superior to that of Islam or any other? You don't think that any one religion has the monopoly on truth?

Absolutely not. They're all questing for the same thing. Of course, each religion has to think that it's the only one that's right, but that just belongs in its origins. Humanity used to think that the end of the universe is over the next mountain, and religion is full of all sorts of prehistoric concepts of history and science – that's part of the clutter that's a problem for our era. They give us loads of nonsense that we can't possibly believe, and if we're not careful we'll lose beautiful buildings, fabulous music, lovely texts, some of the finest reflections of human history on what is right and wrong, written in the most beautiful ways – all because these religions are still carrying clutters of silly teachings.

What you want is an acknowledgement of the mystery, the sacred?

I don't even *want* it, I *have* it. I think my religious childhood partly gave it to me, but I had to leave the rules they gave me to preserve it. This might sound silly, but I sit in my advice bureau and people come to see me with their problems and pain and I love them. I feel I'm doing this service and I have this power because they put it into me with their votes – and I feel like a priest! Then I get up and make speeches, talk about what I think is profoundly right and wrong, and I try to inspire people. We're talking about relevant things, not just some mystery of something in the sky but what's right and wrong and how we could do it one way or the other. I do my sermons. I have my flock. I have my rituals in my party, although some people are trying to get rid of them all. I know some rituals should be updated but I love that part of being a politician. I think it's better than being a priest, because if you could realise it you could make the world finer, and what greater work could you do?

Are you the sort of person who gives thanks?

Well, I do in my mind. I do it when I'm walking along the street or listening to music or swimming – that's when I have my really honest conversations with myself, when I say, 'You're wrong about that, Clare,' or 'You were arrogant,' or 'You were too rude to that person,' or whatever. That's when I make my acts of confession and admit to myself that I'm wrong. Or I say, 'You are so lucky – life is profoundly wonderful and you should just be so grateful that you have all these lovely things.' I do that with myself in my own head, really.

Are those moments like prayer?

. . . I used to pray when I was little, and a lot of prayer is appealing to God to put it right. I mean, when I'm desperate I do sometimes say, 'Well, God, I know you're not there, but if you are, please help me out here.' I have been known to do that, not very often but in my most desperate moments of need . . . I think a lot of it is posited on asking this all-powerful God to do it, but that can't be right. And it can't be that God, who has to be the encapsulation of what is moral and right, would do it if enough people asked him. That would not be a proper way to proceed, so God couldn't behave like that. So I think prayer is this: if in moments of tranquillity and total honesty you encapsulate what is of the deepest importance to you, to give praise or thanks or to appeal for something to happen, you're actually creating moral resolve in yourself.

. . . You speak like somebody who has total faith – in that to believe in goodness, as you do, despite the proof that comes in every day to the contrary, is as big a leap of faith as believing in God.

I've had lots of bad things happen to me and lots of pain, but the whole of my childhood I was given love and kindness, and things that were good were celebrated and honoured all around me . . . My own experience of my own life and human history is that the people who yearn for what is right are the creators of history. The people who just want their own greedy, selfish thing might get it in the short term, but they don't shape anything. To be a human is to be a moral creature.

You speak of religion as being totally about issues of right and wrong, but isn't there more to it than that? Isn't there a philosophical dimension which you're not actually embracing?

I think I am embracing it. I think it is most immediately about right and wrong, but we all have to say what is our place in the universe. What does this concept of God mean? What does our life mean? What does it mean to die? How do we make sense of who we are? What moves us? What inspires us to try again? What does 'spiritual' mean? Is it like when you go by a beautiful mountain or by the sea and it's moving, it lifts your spirit? I think it is, a bit. And very fine music and things that elevate you to another kind of level, that makes you then think more deeply and profoundly about the meaning of life. But that's all part of the religious, too. But the day-to-day of it is: here am I, a human being, within my understandings of life, the universe, beauty, music, death, and I've got to try to be a good person. We have to try . . . If all we are is selfish little beings, it's not worth the struggle.

(1997 conversation)

Meera Syal

Born in Wolverhampton in 1963, Meera Syal went to Manchester University, then embarked on a highly success-ful career as an actress and writer. Her novels include *Anita and Me* (1996) and *Life Isn't All Ha Ha, Hee Hee'* (2001), and her films include *Bhaji on the Beach* (1994). She won a huge following for her appearances in television's long-running, *Goodness Gracious Me*, which she co-wrote, and has won many awards for her work in all fields.

I suppose I do feel that I have a faith of some kind, but it doesn't really fit into any particular recognised category. It's a real mishmash of various influences that I've collected since I was a child. So I don't stick to any particular ritual or religion. But nevertheless, despite all the evidence to the contrary, I do believe that there is something out there and up there that is protective, I'd like to think.

What's the mishmash?

I'm the product of a mixed marriage. My mother is Sikh and my father is Hindu. The two religions aren't that far apart, really. Sikhism was a sort of offshoot and reaction to Hinduism. It removed rigid things like the caste system. In the days when my parents married, it wasn't such a big deal – this was pre-Golden Temple days. Often Hindu families would give their eldest son a Sikh name in respect to the religion. But nevertheless, they are distinct in many ways. So I therefore grew up with Sikh influences from my mother, and sort of vague Hindu influences from my father. He's never been a particularly practising Hindu, because his father was a communist journalist and they were brought up with no religion at all. So I was in the embarrassing position, as I was getting older, having to go to my father and mother and say, 'You haven't taught me one prayer. And when I'm with my Indian friends and they're talking about stuff, I know nothing. And it's your fault.'

So anything I picked up written down about the religions and the rituals, and all that sort of thing, I actually had to do myself, because I wasn't brought up with much prayer in the house. There was a lot of discussion about the meaning of religion, which was very interesting, but it was only Diwali that I remember we celebrated . . .

So there are their influences. I grew up in a mining village in the Midlands, and the centre of all the children's activity was the Wesleyan Methodist church. That was where all the kids went. I went too. So I learned all about the Bible and I did choir practice, and I did the picnics and the plays about religion. That was a big part of my childhood which, to give my parents credit, they never had any problem with, because the one thing that my parents always said was, 'To us, every religion is the same. All the paths lead to the same belief.' And I think the reason that I was never taught organised religion is that my father, particularly, lived through Partition. He was brought up in Lahore, which of course in 1947 became part of Pakistan, so the whole family had to flee across the border. And he saw some dreadful things, many of which he's still not talked about. I think it left a deep, deep impression on him. And I think that because he's seen what people do to each other in the name of formal religion, that's always made him shy away from the formality of it. For him, anyone who says that they're doing such terrible things in the name of God, that's not a god I want to know.

So when you discussed religion at home, was it in terms of values, doing good to people, that sort of thing?

Absolutely. It was about how you treated your fellow human beings and what you expected to get back. How you related to people around you. It's about respect, I think. I was always brought up with a great deal of respect for everybody's beliefs, and I think that's why, as I got older, I then began to learn more about Hinduism and Sikhism, because I was genuinely interested in the roots of the religions. I had Muslim friends at university, so then I found out more about Islam and found that terribly interesting. I got into Buddhism – like everybody did at some stage – because that was one of the world religions I hadn't looked at. I had a Jewish friend at university and found out, gosh, that there are so many parallels between the Indians and the Jews. Found that terribly exciting. So I've literally gone through life gleefully diving in and finding out about different people's faiths, and found so much good in every one.

The big problem that I have with fundamentalist practitioners is that their belief is that their religion is the only one and the right one, and I've never been able to understand that. I think that any path that gives you inner peace and makes you treat human beings in a better way is a good path – I don't care whose path it is. So I find it very problematical that there are people who will happily say, 'Well, of course, you're going to hell because you're not a Christian.' And I've never been able to understand that . . .

The God that you believe in, which is this benevolent power: do you visualise him or her?

Sadly, when I was little, because of my Methodist upbringing it was a big old fat man with a white beard on a cloud, which I realised looked a little bit like Father Christmas, and I wondered if that was the same person. Now I'm older I don't actually see it as a figure: I think it's more of an energy, and without sounding too hippie I think it's in every living thing – in nature, in animals. I'm coming round much more to this Hindu belief that there is a sort of *atman* – soul – that basically passes from life to life to life. And whatever that little spark is, your soul, that is the thing that endures and the body is just a vehicle for that. And that's the energy you feel when you love someone passionately; when you look at your child; when you're with your friends; when you're in the presence of a great piece of music or beautiful nature. Whatever that thing is that floods you and makes you feel like you're connected to a pulse of the universe, that for me is God – whatever that may be.

Your best-selling novel, Life Isn't All Ha Ha, Hee Hee, *starts with a wedding and ends with a funeral. Are those rituals very important?*

I think human beings need ritual to mark the important cycles in life – weddings, births and deaths are what basically we all revolve around. And even people who don't mark them, you'll find, will have their own little rituals plopped into their lives in some way or the other, and they don't even realise that they are . . . I think there are very few people that are brave enough to admit that life may just mean nothing – maybe an existential, unending, pointless exercise. Anyone that's read Becket will know that that is certainly the universe he enacted, and his philosophy was, 'I actually just tell it how it is. Nothing matters. All the things we construct, like relationships and love and where we live and what we eat, are basically just pointless rituals to stave off the great truth that we don't want to admit: that it means nothing.' Most of us don't want to look into that abyss.

The existentialists would argue that we're all just deluded and not brave enough, but I don't think that, and I think that the rituals for many people sustain that really little hidden seed that, yes, there is meaning, and when we do this ritual we are connecting with the bigger meaning and the eternal cycles that influence all of us . . .

When you look at the secular British culture of which you are a part, do you think that there is a void in people when they turn their backs on the idea of God?

I think there's a reason why the societies where faith is still a thread running through them and a part of everyday life – like Muslim or Hindu or Jewish communities – that they do seem somehow more successful in terms of family life, or are more organised in terms of supporting each other. I'm not saying all the time, of course. There's good and bad in everyone, but I think having a map for living is what we need as human beings – even if we don't believe in it, at least it's something to react to. At least it's a set of values to react to.

The reason that all the New Age stuff has made a huge comeback – with astrology and wicca, even, and nature-loving Pagans, sort of things – is this need for people to say, 'We need a faith. However, for me it's not connected with going into a redbrick building. I prefer to worship a tree because that is my faith.' So there is a void, and I think people will fill it, one way or the other.

That goes back so far, doesn't it? For instance, in the pre-Hindu faith, there's the earth goddess, the earth spirit, which is universal throughout the world in primitive faiths.

Absolutely. I do believe that the fundamental energy is female, if it's anything.

So you could imagine yourself as a goddess worshipper?

Absolutely. We all were originally. I firmly believe that the original religions of the entire world were basically female, which were overturned as patriarchy set in . . .

. . . Have you had times in your life, times of personal stress and perhaps grief, where these beliefs have been a consolation?

Yes, I think probably they have. I don't suppose anyone can take away the emotion of the moment. Pain is pain, and people mouthing platitudes doesn't really help. I think you have to face the fact that it's going to hurt and you can't do anything about that. I suppose the thread that pulls you through it is that it isn't always going to be like this, and that one hopes that through the suffering you certainly emerge more compassionate – I think, ironically. All the people that I gravitate to and I feel empathy with are people that have been through similar things. I think if you've experienced pain, particularly personal pain, you never see the world in quite the same complacent way. For example, mental illness. A friend of mine went through a nervous breakdown and I saw her through it. She was an Asian woman. She's now retraining to be a barrister. An amazing woman who, like a phoenix, has risen from an impossible situation. We sit together and we just go, 'God, we will never judge people again.' Particularly me, when I walk down the street and I look around. One third of the population suffers from depression and nobody ever talks about it. And you have this vision in your mind of someone with a cardigan and flappy shoes talking to themselves. She said, 'It's not like that at all. One day you're fine and the next day you've gone.' And really, the line is that close, and you suddenly become aware that life's hard, and the least you can do is try and understand people who are going through stuff. And I think that's what suffering probably does. It should, anyway. It could make some people bitter and closed. I think in some way, though, you have to embrace it.

It has to be endured and seen as a lesson. Is that what you mean?

Without sounding like a hair shirt, yes. I also think you should do it as much as you can to treat yourself and make yourself feel better, and surround yourself with good people, and not be afraid to ask for help, and all those things. I'm not saying you should flagellate yourself and go, 'I deserve this.' Nobody deserves to suffer, that's just the way life is. And I think one should equip one's children to know that there are times when it's going to hurt, but if I can give you all the equipment and the faith and the confidence to deal with it, I hope you'll roll with the punches.

At those bad times, do you ever pray to something?

Yes, I do. It's a bit useless, isn't it, because you think, 'Well, I don't know.' I think it's a very instinctive thing. Most people will pray in those . . . awful life and death situations. The most atheist agnostic will, I think. In my experience of that point of crisis, their instinctive thing is to fall to their knees and go, 'Somebody help me.'

What are the moments when you feel closest to an idea of God?

Different ways, really. For me, it's often through people. It is through the joy I will get from being with the people I love, I think. It's very powerful, particularly for your children – I think more than anything, actually. I think any parent will understand that. And being somewhere that's incredibly beautiful and un-manmade. And again, that's the great thing about children, because they do make you see the world very differently. My daughter will come running in with this amazing 'thing' she's found in the garden, whether it's a beetle or a plant. And you'll go, 'Actually that's an incredible piece of engineering. Who designed that, because it's brilliant?' You get quite overawed about it. It's nice thinking that there is a sort of plan, I suppose. And when you begin to understand that the earth is a delicately balanced living organism and that the minute you imbalance it, all sorts of other things start happening, it's not difficult to believe that there is some sort of system that is to do with yin and yang and balance. And a pattern. We see patterns constantly. You know, psychologists would probably say that's what religion is about. We need to see those patterns to feel reassured that, in the chaos of life, there is something that has meaning and structure, even if we little insects down below can't actually see it.

(2001 conversation)

Amy Tan

Amy Tan's novels have become international best-sellers, with her first, *The Joy Luck Club* (1989) also made into a successful film. Born in Oakland, California, she has published articles and children's books as well as *The Kitchen God's Wife* (1992), *The Hundred Secret Senses* (1995) and *The Bonesetter's Daughter* (2000), each of which has met with critical acclaim.

Your four novels have at their core a quest for cultural identity, within a powerful network of family history. So let us start with some personal history . . .

My father was a Baptist minister, as were my grandfather and all my aunts and uncles – twelve of them – all evangelists in China. Later on they emigrated to different parts of the world, but all started off with these very deeply held Christian beliefs. I believe that the origins of that have to do with schooling and missionary-related programmes during the turn of the century. All of my grandfather's letters to his children were written in English, and they always had a lot to do with religion, so all of the family became very religious.

And what about your mother?

My mother was a typical Chinese woman from Shanghai, meaning that she had an eclectic background of beliefs which I call 'ultimate pragmatism'. She went to a Catholic girls' school that was Western in tradition, but also believed in Buddhism, ancestor worship, ghosts, curses – whatever worked.

It's a very rich mix. Did your father, with his devout Christianity, approve of that other tradition?

Certainly the beliefs that my mother had, particularly in ghosts, were kept hidden from me, and she didn't speak about them in the family until after my father died – well, actually, when my father and my brother became ill with brain tumours. That's when she believed that the curses had fully come into force in our family, and so she couldn't help but speak about them. She started asking what we had done in our past – whether there were ancestors who were unhappy with us, or if our house had been built on cursed land with bad feng shui. And all these different beliefs came out. It was quite a shock to me.

But up to that point, had your upbringing been very rigidly Baptist? Was it narrow in that sense?

You had to believe in your faith completely, meaning you accepted the doctrine of the Baptist religion – that you were reborn once you took Jesus Christ as your lord and saviour, and 'Whosoever believeth in me shall have everlasting life'. That was the promise, that you would then go on to eternity and have this kind of peace. And then there were certain rules of behaviour which also accompanied it, like no swearing, no drinking – you had to behave in a certain way. We prayed every day, certainly, and I went to church almost every day. There was an activity – say, a youth activity, choir, Bible study, prayer breakfast, things like that. So I was very, very involved with the Church. And I used to go to the beach on Saturday, to Santa Cruz, and try to recruit children – other students, teenagers lying in bikinis kissing boys – to come and discover a better life through the Baptist religion. I did manage to get a few of my friends to come.

I think it was a good period of my life, to have gone through that experience of absolute faith where it's a truth that's handed to you, because then I can compare it to the other, when I lost that faith so completely. When I lost my father and my brother, I realised that I could not trust in any set of beliefs or absolute truths that had simply been handed to me. I had to ask questions too. Now, I'm not saying that those beliefs of the Baptist religion are wrong or harmful, or anything like that. But simply that I as a person cannot have a set of beliefs just given to me, which then become part of my psyche. I have to discern what the truth is for *me*. And whatever my truth is, it's not one I would try to impose on anyone else, because the questions are very, very particular, very specific to me. That's what I think. Also fiction writing is very specific and particular. Each story is its own universe, its own cosmology.

The harrowing story of your mother's early life was the inspiration for The Joy Luck Club *and* The Kitchen God's Wife. *There's an overwhelming sense in all your work that the generations are compelled to revisit old traumas, like a Greek tragedy. Were you brought up to believe in that sort of destiny?*

I suppose it was always there under the surface. It wasn't talked about, as in: 'Here is what happened in the past. Here is the history of your family and this is the tradition that you need to carry on.' In fact, I knew nothing about my family's past. I didn't know that my grandmother had been a concubine, that she had killed herself, that my mother had seen this happen. I didn't know that my grandfather had been raised in a missionary school.

The past for me started in 1949, only a few years before I was born, because 1949 was the year my parents came to the United States. And it was also a period of time in the United States where there was a lot of paranoia about communism, which meant you really did not refer to a past in China. So, essentially, I did not discover the real past of my family until much later in life – around the time, probably, that I started thinking of writing fiction.

When your mother revealed to you all this great depth of traditional belief – some people might call it superstition – did you feel that you had been deprived of something all those years?

Oh, I didn't feel deprived. I felt I was being assaulted with her beliefs and I was horrified! Anything that my mother had to say to me sounded like gibberish and was frightening – all her talk about ghosts. I realised later that she had always believed I had a talent in speaking to ghosts from the time I was a little child. She would make little remarks to me, like, 'You see them, don't you?' or 'Tell me where they are, don't be afraid.'

Was the idea of ghosts in any way connected in your mind to the Christian idea of life after death?

I think there is a connection. It's the sense that there is a spirit and the spirit is benevolent, or certainly not malevolent, and it's larger than any individual. That works with the concept of a god. It also links with a concept of – not so much forgiveness, in the Christian sense, but compassion. And so I make it my goal to learn about this notion of compassion, about a complete empathy with people, which is, I think, another way of saying 'love'. This emotion of love we can't measure, it has no dimension that we can scientifically prove, just as we can't scientifically prove anything about an afterlife. That is something that I can hang on to and say, 'Yes, I believe this,' because I find intuitive emotional truth in that, day to day, in both real life and in my fiction.

It's very tolerant and all-encompassing, isn't it? And to that extent, forgiving. Because you are projecting yourself into imaginary lives. I'm thinking, in that sense it's very different from the guilt which is at the heart, perhaps, of those two other traditions: the Baptist and also the traditional Chinese. Lot of guilt flowing around there.

A lot of guilt and a lot of fear are associated with the Baptist religion. I have to say, my notions of the Baptist religion go back more than thirty-five years, so it may have changed, but back then there was definitely a notion of Hell. If you did not abide by these rules, if you did not believe in Jesus, if you did certain things, but particularly if you weren't baptised you would go to Hell. And that's why it was so important to save other people. In my mother's beliefs there was a sense of fear that there might have been something done in the past that offended somebody – a ghost. And that this ghost was now going to come back and harm you.

You're perpetually haunted by these possibilities?

My mother was suicidal because her mother had killed herself and she had witnessed it. This was also part of the psyche of many Chinese women of that period. The suicide rate was very, very high, and continues to be very high. It's double what it is in most countries, and in most countries suicide rates are higher among men than they are among women – except in China. You have the tradition of a belief in anger, a vengeful ghost, combined with the notion of suicide as not just an act of despair, but an act of revenge. The idea was that you would come back as a ghost and you would exact these penalties against the people who had wronged you, and people knew that. Everybody else had the same set of beliefs . . .

We should revisit that terrible time when your father and your brother died in one year.

Six months apart.

When you said that at this point you lost your faith and you didn't want any longer to have a set of beliefs handed down to you, were you also saying, 'There cannot possibly be this Christian God, and this Christian message of love and Jesus, because this can happen'?

It was not so much against God. It was against spoon-fed religion. I had believed so completely that I actually thought the miracle would happen. I felt the miracle had been promised to me, that my father and my brother would live. If I had enough faith, they would live. Of course, maybe I didn't understand it properly, as a child, but I believed that all great things could happen if only your faith was great enough. And I think my father believed that, too, all the way until the moment he died – that somehow he would be saved if his faith was great enough . . .

In my case, being fifteen years old, I was at that ripe age where I would become a cynic about anything. So religion was a prime thing for me to reject. And I had all the reasons to reject it. I had been promised the miracle of my father and brother surviving this terrible disease and they didn't. They died.

. . . It made me think, 'Well, what is it that bolsters our faith? What is the importance of faith? What's the importance of hope?' For a while, it made me angry, this notion of faith and hope, and it wasn't until I was much older, when I started to write fiction, that I was able to revisit that period and see that I had a sense of anger from disillusionment about faith, but that faith and hope do serve very important functions and are essential to many people. They are as important as believing in love. But it's for the individual to find what those reasons are . . .

. . . Here in San Francisco, people practise a whole range of beliefs, from feng shui through to conventional religion in many different forms. Sometimes people will mock the sort of ragbag of New Age belief – but do you think that people need to believe in something, so it doesn't really matter what they latch on to?

I think people can't help but believe in something. We all have a sense of how the world works. And again, I would say that if you ask a person, 'Do you have any particular religious beliefs?' and they reply, 'No,' they may not have them organised in their heads. But if you were to ask, 'Well, do you believe in Fate? Do you believe in destiny? Do you believe in luck? Do you believe in coincidences? Do you believe that each thing leads to another, concatenation of events? Or do you believe in total chaos?' they will answer yes or no. If you ask enough questions of people, you find that they *do* have beliefs.

I think the interesting thing today is looking at those who have beliefs which so control their lives and the lives of others that it becomes dangerous. I was raised with the idea: 'Whosoever believeth in me shall have everlasting life.' But there are other people who are saying: 'Whosoever believeth in whatever *this* religion is – and what

I tell you to do – you're going to have everlasting life, if you follow these rules.' All of us have to pay attention to how we impose our ideas on others in the belief that the consequences will be better for the rest of the world. After 11 September we all know what this means. As Americans, we can see how our views on how to improve the world – which perhaps we have imposed on others – have led to a backlash. Because others answer us back: 'Well, *our* beliefs are the ones that should be in operation for the good of the whole world.' It's interesting too, the notions of suicide as a form of revenge, when you get to come back and exact a penalty from people. Even post-11 September, I don't think Americans really understand suicide *not* as an act of despair but as revenge. But if you've been raised in a culture where suicide is thought of very differently, then you see what a very frightening and powerful tool it can be . . .

As a writer, I don't have any general beliefs that I would ever want to give to anybody, any bits of advice, any absolute truths.

Whom do you turn to when you seek answers?

I turn to fiction, but within fiction there is a form of meditation that happens. It's thinking a great deal about moral questions, and about how the world works, and what is my place in the world, and how do I affect the world? I don't mean that in a grandiose sense, of me the fiction writer, I mean my actions as an individual. Each of our actions may have some consequence in these minute ways that might spiral. I believe the purpose of life is to ask these questions and find the answers – and it's fascinating.

Standing in between two cultures, as you do, and being this even-handed – I'm wondering now, if your mother was to walk into this room, would you say to her that actually she was right, there was a lot of truth in the things that she said about ghosts and spirits?

I am in communication with my mother all the time. I don't have to say it to her. She knows. I still get a lot of help and a lot of insight from her. She was not a perfect person, and she knows that that's OK for me. She was enormously hopeful. She had an enormous capacity to take in all possibilities, and that is a gift she gave me.

When you think about what you have to do as a fiction writer, you have to be open to all possibilities, you cannot have a limited point of view. You have to consider everyone's point of view, and all the things that they could possibly believe in. So I feel very lucky that I grew up in a family that was traditionally religious in a Western sense, and also eclectic in my mother's sense. It's a creative mix: finding what works for each situation.

(2002 conversation)

Joanna Trollope

One of the most popular novelists in Britain, Joanna Trollope is the author of over twenty-five books, including best-sellers like *The Choir* (1988), *The Rector's Wife* (1991) and *Other People's Children* (1998), as well as historical novels under the pseudonym Caroline Harvey.

In your novel The Choir, *there's an interesting little passage which I thought would serve as a starting point for this discussion. It says: ' "There's no need to say anything when you pray," the Dean had heard Bishop Roberts say at a recent confirmation in the city, "just take time to look at God and let him look at you. That's all." ' Is it as easy as that?*

No, nothing like! That's incredibly idealistic. You have to remember I was probably trying to get into the bishop's head, and you know how bishops always want to make faith seem an incredibly easy, accessible thing for people. 'You don't have to work at this, dear. It's as easy as picking up a can of beans. You just lie there and it will happen to you if your mind is receptive.' I don't actually think it works like that at all.

Well, let's seek something a little bit more precise. Do you ever take time to look at God, and if so, what do you see?

I don't take time to look. I take time to suspend myself a bit. The older I get, the less certain I get about organised faith in any way. This doesn't seem to be troubling – perhaps it should be. But I am conscious of a dimension – you could call it a spiritual dimension, if you like. I *think* I think there's a God. I certainly think there's a capacity in all of us for something extraordinary and wonderful which is beyond just creative ability. So I suppose there are moments when I try and be very still, if you see what I mean, and just see what happens. Empty vessel, really: see what pours in.

I'm in a state of hoping – always. But I'm in a state of hoping about most aspects of life; you know, whether emotional, intellectual, financial or whatever. I don't think I want a moment on the road to Damascus. I don't want a blinding vision. I would rather have a mounting sense of reassurance – not so much for myself but for dear ones, for loved ones. I want to know they are going to be safe.

Safe from what?

Too many agonies and perils, too many disappointments. And although you can't shield anybody from disappointment, you can somehow help them to have the equipment to deal with it, and I always hope some extra force will assist me in helping them, or even just directly help them. This all sounds extremely undefined, because it is. I think if you'd asked me all these questions twenty years ago, I would have been able to reply in a much more brisk and orthodox manner . . .

I was born quietly, peacefully, into the Church of England. My grandfather, in whose rectory I was born, in the Cotswolds, was what now would be regarded as an absolute dinosaur: he was a hunting parson. He'd been a bush brother in Western Queensland in the First World War, and so he did everything in the parish on horseback he possibly could. You know, taking communion to sick parishioners, delivering the parish magazines – all on horseback. He took communion with spurs under his cassock. It was all rather dashing. He was a tremendous part of my childhood – a man of shining, simple spiritual integrity; without any question a really good fellow.

And that, in a way, was easy. I was always rather a line-toer. I was the kind of child who did homework on the night you were expected to do it. And this sort of sad and suburban orthodoxy flowed over into all areas of life, including faith.

But I think one of the interesting things about getting older is developing a confidence in yourself, and this includes a confidence about your spiritual beliefs: that you don't *have* to believe things. You're allowed to question without the world falling to pieces.

So – a confidence in not being confident.

Yes. That it's perfectly all right not to be certain.

Do you remember the stage in your life when the old certainties – the certainties of your grandfather, the certainties presumably of your parents, too – started to ebb away? Can you place it in your life pattern?

I think it took years, and I'm sure it was tied up with the disintegration of two marriages. You know, that makes you look at things in a cool and dispassionate way, and do a lot of internal investigation. And of course, the female propensity is always, in these circumstances, to feel one is entirely to blame – this cocktail of guilt and anxiety that we're assumed to stagger about with. And I found that the Church itself was not as helpful as I might have wished it to be. I mean, that may well be the simple business of not talking to the right priest when I needed a prop and stay, and not finding the right priest to talk to . . .

I wanted to ask you whether you feel that in writing about people who have troubles – all your characters live very messy lives, and very many in the shadow of the Church in some way – you yourself are helping them in a way?

I feel very diffident about that. I'd love to feel it was the case. I daren't, because it seems a bit presumptuous. What do I know, really? I can only sort of suggest. I would like people to feel less guilty about their reaction to the things that happen in life. I mean, I firmly believe that most people get life wrong out of muddle and not out of malevolence. I think most people are earnestly trying to do the right thing, and that what is so extraordinary is how many people get through their lives with so much stoicism. We hear so much about the victim culture, and people spilling the beans about their pain. That's a tiny minority who spill the beans. Most people get on with their pain and don't offload it on to other people. And I would like to feel that the novels sometimes hold a bit of a hand out to them.

In The Rector's Wife, *Anna, the rector's wife whose husband has just failed to get his promotion within the Church, says, 'What a thing to do to someone who serves you.' You go on, 'God said nothing. He held himself aloof.' I should think a lot of people would identify with that because when they seek help – either from God or his earthly representatives – they find an aloofness.*

. . . And a curious intolerance. I am a tremendous fan of the Christian virtues of compassion and tolerance, but I would like to see a bit more of it in the Church, quite frankly . . .

I don't think it's universally that bad. But I think its public image is, to say the least, unfortunate, and gives a rather excluding air. It's almost as if 'if you won't toe the line, if you won't be sufficiently evangelical, if you won't be sufficiently conventional, then we're awfully sorry, but I'm afraid the unwritten law says you can't join in'. And the whole Church should be . . . I don't know, almost more ragged – you know, less ritualised. All this tremendous kerfuffle in Rome recently has shown what happens when a church, or an orthodox faith, becomes absolutely fossilised, and a church begins to think in terms of centuries rather than the week it's living in. And the ritual begins to take the place of the heart. It's the heart that's missing, I think. That's what I feel.

And do you think that's why people don't go to church? Or that people like you and I are perhaps overestimating the desire for spirituality in people at large?

I don't think you can overestimate it. I think what the Church is lacking is a kind of emotional intelligence. It's just not being imaginative enough about how hard people are trying, and how tremendously lost so many of them feel – the whole business of faith, you know. That's why the bishop in the novel talks in this rather cosy and domesticated way. Of course it's difficult, but I don't think it's impossible.

I remember reading somewhere that you said you often argue with God when you're out walking your dog or whatever. What do you argue with him about?

Nothing very sophisticated. It would be about suffering, particularly the suffering of the very young or the vulnerable.

The problem of pain, in C.S. Lewis's phrase?

Precisely. The problem of pain. And the problem of psychological pain. The problem of people learning to live with themselves, to be reconciled with themselves. We're stumbling towards it, with all this rather unattractive modern jargon about self-worth and self-esteem, which is a pity and clouds the issue. I think there's a failure to understand how hard a lot of people find just living with themselves; that the reconciliation to self is where it's all got to start – not a great, elaborate public forgiveness, but an acceptance that this is a universal pattern of complication. We're all in this boat together. There isn't the Church on the one hand and the flock on the other. The Church and the flock are actually in the same boat.

But do you think that it's God's fault – if we're assuming that there is a God . . . that people feel at odds with themselves and with the world?

This is part of my own struggle. Because although I feel people are, to a large degree, neglected by the Church, I also feel . . . no, I'll rephrase that: I also *believe* that we have free will. Without question, we have free will. The penalty of having free will is that you have to accept the consequences of the decisions you make using your free will. So you can't then, having made a choice, turn round and shake your fist at the heavens and say, 'Look what you've made me do.' That's where my own conflicts come. This is where I find the reconciliation so difficult, because I can't make intellectual sense of it, and I can't – yet (maybe I never will, I'll see) – hold my nose and jump. I can't do that leap.

I remember talking to the grandson of two scientific Nobel Prize-winners, and I said to him, 'Do you think, when your grandfathers made their great discoveries, there was a moment in their great discoveries where there was a leap of faith?' And he said, 'Oh, without question, with both of them.' Both of them got to their conclusion and then looked back and worked out the sequence of how they'd got there. And I suppose, in an ideal world, the leap into faith would be the same. I just can't quite do it. I don't know if it's something to do with control. It fascinates me. I'll go on worrying away at it.

Because you want to be in control.

I like being in control. I feel safer being in control.

Do you ever pray?

Yes. Quite eloquently – usually on behalf of somebody who I feel needs it. I mean, the baby of great friends of my elder daughter has just been terrifyingly ill, and that required real primary school prayers from me, in that kind of language, with a kind of force-fulness. I'm a bit nervous about praying on my own behalf, for basic things like huge improvements in character and so on! But I'm not sure I quite have the nerve to ask for things directly.

But you would say, 'Please, God, make this child better'?

Oh, without question, yes.

And in that moment are you looking at God? You're looking to be listened to?

I'm *shouting* to be listened to. I'm making demands. All I'm trying to say is, I'm not visualising. I'm certainly making demands. And then I think to myself, 'Goodness. These habits of prayer and faith die very hard, don't they?' They're still all lying about in my subconscious . . .

Because we all battle very manfully on our own, I think. I think most people are very conscious of their ultimate solitariness. And this is, I suppose, the only – as it were – hand that you can hold on to occasionally. And being human, we need in some sense not exactly to visualise it, but to summon it up.

It all comes back to feeling there is something in all of us that is not necessarily terrestrial. There's something that makes even the most banal of people capable of moments, thoughts of glory, sheer glory. It's one of the things I always love about the Renaissance, for all its drawbacks: this belief in the capacity of the human mind to explore and to achieve.

Does that give you solace in the face of all the contrary evidence, all the evil . . . ?

Yes, oh yes. But you see, we *hear* about the wickedness, don't we, because the wickedness has drama? There is a black glamour about Lucifer that there isn't about a god. So that fills centre stage, because that's the noisy child with the trumpet in the foreground. And goodness can be very dull. People don't write about goodness much because it loses its essence on the page. So we focus on the opposite, then inevitably we come to believe there's more of it – just because it's making more fuss.

So when you are in extremis – *we talked about, for instance, when your marriages broke up – and you said you did go to the Church for help and didn't receive it, is it possible for you at those dark times just to contemplate a kind of universal goodness, and find solace in that? Does that help at all?*

Yes, because the goodness was very evident in other people who came to my rescue. And anyway, I'm not free of blame. I perhaps didn't try hard enough. I didn't go and seek other people in the Church. I made one or two attempts; they were unsatisfactory. I didn't persevere and I should have. I'd like to be fair about it. But other people displayed extraordinary support, and maybe that is God-like. That is God working in mysterious ways, through humanity in general. And most unexpected. You will know this yourself from crises in your own life, that people who rode to your rescue were often the most astonishing surprises to you.

But back to this moment of stillness. I think, too, in times of trouble, I've learned to kind of hold myself in reserve. One of the things about getting older is that you know the storm clouds. They'll always be there, but they're not going to overwhelm you. They will pass a little. The sun will come out again. Rather like a wounded cat going into a corner and just being in a dark, quiet place until it's better: I find I can do that psychologically . . .

. . . Returning to that extract I started with, and the exchange within it. I know it's very cosy, but it's interesting because it says, 'Let him look at you.' It just occurs to me: what do you hope your God sees when he looks at you?

I like the image of the shepherd. I've always liked the image of the shepherd. So I would like the feeling that he was looking out for me to some extent. I would find that very consoling. And I would like *him* to feel that I've done something, at least, towards exercising some of the talents I've got. I don't know: seven out of ten would do!

I know that you're a great admirer of many Victorian novelists, including your distant relative, 'that Trollope'. And this idea of living a good life was very, very important, wasn't it? Is it important to you?

Yes, I think it is. Trying to live perhaps a decent life – not necessarily a respectable life. The British are very good at confusing respectability and decency. But I think a decent life, by which I would mean one that took sufficient consideration of other people. I've got a quotation from Philip Toynbee on my desk, which I absolutely love, and it goes: 'The definition of moral progress is the realisation that other human beings are fully as human as oneself.' So if I got a divine tick for that, or even half a tick, I would be very pleased. Relieved.

You feel as if you're on trial?

I think I always will.

Where does that come from?

Who knows? Childhood? Being an eldest? Being the genetic bundle of DNA I am? Who knows? I don't know. But there's a kind of anxiety there which I've got used to. It may not be particularly comfortable sometimes, but I have got used to it. I know how to deal with it most of the time. But it keeps you striving.

And I tell you the other thing – and this may be where faith kicks in – it keeps you remembering about humility. You may have done fine, but you haven't done *that* fine, and other people perhaps have done much better. Just keeps your head screwed on straight.

Do you think there's part of your brain which is always remembering your old grandfather's ringing tones from the pulpit, with this kind of message of humility?

His was different. His was more a beacon of extremely benevolent faith in humankind. That was more the message.

166

That is the message of your books, which is that people will get into trouble, live their lives, pray to a God who may or may not be listening, get cross, and somehow muddle through.

And behave badly – but not be damned for that.

Forgiveness is an important part . . .

Incredibly important. It's the one thing that always goes on. It's like there always being time to repent. It's never too late to forgive. And it's far better to do it. It's the only constructive way to go on. It doesn't corrode you. It's one of the few emotions that doesn't. The few means at your disposal of putting down the burdens that do corrode you – the angers and the resentments and disappointments and rejections – that everybody has all the time. There's the most wonderful bit in Anthony Trollope's autobiography where he says – I'm paraphrasing wildly – 'My landscape isn't that of the sort of great operatic emotion.' I think he was thinking of Tolstoy, whom he hugely admired. He said, 'My task as a novelist is to chronicle those little daily lacerations upon the spirit.' And that, of course, is what people have to bear on the daily journey to work, in work, at home, on a failed holiday. The spirit is lacerated at every turn. And to behave decently through all that is an extraordinary achievement, and I still think vast numbers of people manage to do it superbly but don't get the credit.

With or without the help of a personal God.

Yes. Isn't it funny, this phrase 'a personal God'? I'd much rather mine was shared! I don't want one of my own. It's too much responsibility! Do you remember those Japanese toys you had to look after, otherwise they died? It's rather like: if you don't pay attention to your personal God, he'll just push off!

When the chips are down, do you think you are more devout or more sceptical?

I don't think sceptical's quite the right word. I think I have a capacity for devotion, but I keep holding whole areas of myself back. It's a kind of holding in reserve rather than doubting. I'm perfectly prepared to have it all spread out in front of me, but I am not perfectly prepared to commit. Sceptical – I think – is really the answer, isn't it?

(2002 conversation)

Mary Warnock

Baroness Warnock had a distinguished academic career at Oxford University, and has played a key role in shaping public policy on matters of education and ethics. She was the Chairman of the Committee of Inquiry into Human Fertilisation and of the Advisory Committee on Animal Experiments, and has published books on education and philosophy.

Let's just start with a definition, no matter how loose it may be. How do you describe yourself, if asked, in relation to religious faith?

I say that I am a member of the Church of England, which is true, and I am a fairly regular church attender – for various, slightly complicated reasons such as supporting the village church and going to listen to the music. But I'm definitely a member of the Church of England, so that's where I'd start.

. . . I think I question absolutely everything – if I'm supposed to take what I recite in the creed literally. I think my position really is that I like the Church of England, I like the Christian religion, and that's rather different from actually believing in it. I'm a great believer in the Church, actually, as the instrument of continuity, and the

169

existence of the Church makes me think that I belong to an organisation that has roots in the beginning of Christianity and goes trickling on through its history. And the actual words and the music that people have used for generations are very important to my view of being a member of the Church. So the continuity of the Church is something I value extremely highly. But, of course, I don't believe that everything that one is taught to say in church is literally true . . .

Were you brought up a Christian?

In one way, very much so. My mother came of a family which converted to Christianity, or had converted to Christianity, and her mother became an intensely pious Christian, having been an intensely pious Jew before. My mother was a great churchgoer, but what she actually believed I think would be quite difficult to ascertain. But certainly I was brought up to go to church.

And then I went to a school that was intensely pious, and I took rather against – not religion, but the people who were religious. I was an intellectual snob as a child, and I really couldn't bear the holy people.

. . . Curiously enough, I don't think my attitude to religion has really changed very much since I was conscious. Because I've always loved the words. I loved the psalms, I loved the hymns. I have a sister who is just older than me. We were brought up very much as a pair, and she had an absolute fascination for words, so before I could even read or know anything about it, she used to come back from school with these wonderful words about our 'mediator and *labricate*' (as she used to say!) and the 'holy *parakeet*' – and all kind of wonderful ideas that we used to get from the hymns and the psalms.

It's very interesting when you speak about religion in this way. To me it sounds so aesthetic, as if it is actually part of an aesthetic; it's the beauty, the building, the words – not so much a philosophy.

Oh, you're right. I couldn't possibly distinguish between the aesthetic and the religious. If you read a poem that you really like . . . I'm deeply interested in Wordsworth, and I think *The Prelude* is one of the most marvellous poems that ever there was, and when I read parts of *The Prelude* I just feel that there is a truth in this, and I can go on exploring. I think my attitude to religion is the same: there's a truth in it that I can go on exploring.

It's interesting – you talk about the beauty and the richness of literature or music, but for someone like Bertrand Russell, who hated religion, those things themselves are evidence of man, not of God, of the beauty of man, of man's spirit.

I think I'd agree with that, that it's after all only humans who tangle either with aesthetics or with religion, as far as we know. And I think the difference between man and other animals is the possession by mankind of imagination (or I would *call* that difference the possession of imagination) – to be able to comprehend things beyond the present. Because one of the things that religion is essentially concerned with is continuity between the past and the future. It's extremely important to me that continuity with the Jewish religion is kept on in the Church by the use of the psalms, because of the concept there of God . . . before any humans, the mountains and the seas were created by God, and this will go on from generation to generation for ever, which seems to me the sort of feeling that one is seeking from religion, a feeling of continuity with the whole universe.

I think the only difference with its being religion, rather than some other aesthetic attitude, is that in religion one is permitted – indeed, encouraged – to experience a sense of gratitude for being a member of the universe, a part of the universe; and that seems to me to be what's meant by saying that there's a person – God – to whom one can be grateful. Because if one just thinks of oneself, as Russell did, as just one of the bits of the universe that happens to be quite bright, that's it. There's no one to be grateful to. I think I feel quite keenly a sense of gratitude.

And you move then from a feeling of religion as observance, ritual, continuity, words, music, buildings, and that beauty, to a sense of man in the universe with, presumably, moral responsibilities to it. Which leads us to the ethics of Christianity.

I think that the fact that humans are so much brighter than other animals and have these great imaginative capacities to take in the thought of the universe as a whole and the past and the future – the fact that humans have this does give them a responsibility for behaving well and, perhaps particularly, behaving well about the future. I mean, we do know how much damage we can do to things. I think it's quite easy to think of the metaphors of religion – the life of the world to come, for example – as metaphors of what will happen to the world when we personally have disappeared.

I think this attitude to religion has been essentially to do with reflecting on being part of the universe. It does make the question of death, for example, rather less important. Everybody dies, but after they're dead things will go on. So, in a way, people have a responsibility for what happens next. Now that used to be put in the metaphor of heaven and hell: if you behave well, you'll go to heaven; if you behave badly, you'll roast in hell. Nobody believes that now, and nobody could believe it. For one thing, nobody could believe that individuals persist after death, but that doesn't mean that they don't have responsibility and that what they do now does make a difference.

Have you studied the moral imperatives of other great world religions?

No, I'm not particularly interested in other religions because I really do have this kind of love affair with the English church liturgy, and as far as I am concerned that is what I mean by religion. The other reason I love the Church of England is that it's so flexible and doesn't really lend itself to fundamentalism, and I'm terrified of fundamentalism, whether Christian, Muslim, Jewish or any other kind. It demands a kind of fanatical obedience which is contrary to the best that humans are able to do, which is think and make up their own minds.

As a philosopher, someone who studies reason and all forms of truth, you might say it is actually nonsense – that a whole religion could be founded upon a myth.

I think I've always been very much interested in mythology as a form of truth, and I think, therefore, that I never thought of Christianity as literally true. I think I've always been much impressed in every way by the philosopher Kant, and he said that all of the language of religion is metaphorical. To think otherwise, he said, would be the greatest anthropomorphism. And I think I've always thought that. So, therefore, one takes this whole language of religion and begins to see – sometimes in rather surprising ways – how the metaphors contained in it are truthful, sometimes difficult to do without.

I'll give you one example: when I was working on the committee concerned with educating children who were handicapped, in the late 1970s, we had to start right from the beginning to say *why* we were urging government to spend money on educating even children who were so severely handicapped that actually they would never be able to live an independent life, they'd never be other than a burden on the state. Why should we want to educate them? And I think I then recognised that if this committee within which I was working had been a committee of Christians, it would have been very easy to say, 'Because we're all God's children.' And that metaphor I actually find helpful, because the relationship between ourselves and these exceedingly disadvantaged children is illuminated for me by the idea that we are all equal in the eyes of God. Of course, this was not a wholly religious committee and it was impossible to present a report to government, to ministers, saying, 'You've got to spend money on this because we're all God's children.' Nevertheless, I felt that this was a metaphor which, to me, was difficult to replace, actually. One had got to say something else about the compassion that one ought to feel, the equality that one ought to assert between oneself and even the most damaged other humans. The quick way to do this was through religion.

In your book Imagination, *you wrote of 'the belief that there's more in our experience of the world than can possibly meet the unreflecting eye'. And you went on: 'This kind of belief may be referred to as the feeling of infinity.' Could you enlarge on that a little – what you mean by the feeling of infinity?*

I suppose that everybody who's been moved by reading Shakespeare or listening to some music, or indeed, very often, in some natural surroundings when walking or riding, has been moved by – not exactly immortal longings, but the feeling that there is enormously more significance in what one sees or hears than one can immediately take in.

Is that feeling the same feeling, or the stage before what one might call the experience of the sacred?

My own opinion would be that it's the very same feeling, but in the context of religion there is very strongly added to it the thought that this has a long history, that you're not the only person who's had this sentiment.

It's interesting – I see three stages here, if you like. I see a feeling of infinity leading on to – not being the same as – the sense of the sacred. Because the feeling of infinity could just be a sense of mystical oneness without necessarily a sense of the numinous, the holy, the special. And then another stage, which is where I find I can't go, which is the idea of God. Do you see what I mean? I don't see them as the same.

I understand what you're saying. I think that the stage in between that used to be rather engagingly put as regarding nature as the language of God, or the book in which one reads God. I think the connection between natural phenomena – the mountains, or whatever it is that one is moved by and given the sense of infinity – the connection between that and the idea of a god is very close. The philosopher Spinoza thought that nature and God were just two ways of referring to the same thing: the whole of the universe – *natura* or *deus*, it didn't matter which you said – of both of which humans were part. Now that is a kind of idea which I think could lead on to the notion that if you talk about God, you're talking about that which is utterly permanent and to which human beings, through being natural objects, are somehow connected. And I think that is what I would regard as the crucial metaphor of talking about 'one God'. But if you said, 'Well, all right, tell me a bit more about this God,' I couldn't possibly do that. I don't know anything about it at all, and I entirely agree, again, with Kant that you can't possibly prove either that God does exist or that God doesn't exist. It simply depends how you're using the expression.

I like the phrase which Dietrich Bonhoeffer used: 'A God-shaped blank in the soul.' This word 'soul' fascinates me, and I'd like to know if you can define it. But just before you do that: a rationalist like Russell – a philosopher like yourself but with a passionate hatred of religion – used the word 'soul' with a poetic intensity again and again in his writing. What's going on there?

Well, I think the word 'soul' causes me great difficulty, because I believe – and I think I would say I *know* – that everything that humans are capable of in the way of thought, language, imagination, is to be traced to certain functions of different parts of the brain. So humans are very complex physical objects, with brains that work in ways that we don't yet fully understand. But the brain gives rise to all that I have been talking about as imagination, and obviously gives rise to the birth of language, without which one couldn't even conceive of religion or imagination or anything else.

So what is there that is the soul? The answer, I suppose, would be that it's the collection of thoughts and feelings which concentrate on these numinous senses of mystery or the sacred that we've just been talking about. That is to say, you're right to think that these two ideas interlock. If anybody wants to talk about the soul, then what they're talking about is that way of thinking and feeling that humans are capable of. And if one says of somebody that they had no soul, I suppose one would mean that they thought of nothing except the immediate future before them, the immediate next meal or where to get their money from, and never had any of these sensations, or had suppressed them from childhood so that they wouldn't be excited by the concepts of either the arts or religion or even the sense that one could go on talking about something for ever. That wouldn't strike them.

The idea of soul leads us inescapably towards considering death. Do you think that the need to believe is inextricably bound up with the inevitability of death?

I find this quite difficult. The older I get, the less death seems to me particularly important, in the sense that I suppose that we all know that everybody dies, though when one's young one doesn't think about it very much unless it's brought to one's attention by some awful tragedy. That individual people die doesn't seem to me to make very much difference to the – as it were – eternity of the universe and the sort of things we've been talking about as mysterious and continuous. So that although I die, something else goes on. I do believe that this is part of the need that we have, not so much for religion as for formalised religion. I believe that church services, funeral services, kinds of ritual, are very good at symbolising that things go on, even though individual people sadly die – or not so sadly if they're ready for death.

I don't believe that the notion of eternity need have anything to do with individual persons living for ever, because we know they don't. But it does have something to do with things going on, the universe going on. And maybe some people will have made a difference to the way things go on after they die. Maybe everybody does in a limited way, through their children or their pupils or whoever it is. But I believe that this notion of the world being continuous with the past, the history of the world continuing into the future, is of far more importance than any individual death in the world.

It's a profound consolation.

I suppose it's a consolation. It's not a consolation if somebody you love is facing death. I'm sure it's not a consolation then. But I think when thinking about one's own death, it's certainly a consolation.

That's what I meant. Do you think about death?

At the moment I think about death quite a lot, simply because I'm on a select committee in the House of Lords considering euthanasia. So it's very much at the front of my mind at the moment, and I certainly have supplied to my GP, who's a great friend, an advanced directive about how I don't want to be resuscitated and I do want to be allowed to die without heroic measures being taken, and all that kind of thing. I think that is a great help to doctors, actually, because it means that they may well do what they have an instinctive wish to do, which is to ease the passing of people, but which at the moment, as the law stands, they can't do without great risk to themselves. So I have been thinking a lot about death, and I find myself curiously indifferent to my own death provided that I don't become a great burden to my children.

You said that you have always doubted, and go on doubting, many of the things which formed Christian belief for a lot of people – the detail of faith. What about the idea of resurrection and salvation? In personal terms, do you feel that you'll meet your God face to face?

No. I don't know what that even means. I simply believe that when I die I shall be as other animals are when they die, but that presumably there will be other people who will take my place. I regard myself as destined to become part of the natural environment, as I am now. So, when I'm dead, my body will be part of the natural environment. All I could mean by meeting my God face to face would be simply lying down and dying and being part of nature.

Back to that equation of God with nature . . . And what about your soul?

Well, if I had been Wordsworth or Milton or Shakespeare, then there's no doubt that my soul would live on. But as I'm not, it won't. Although, I suppose as long as my children remember me, they may think they've got a picture of what sort of person I really was, just as I have of my mother, and I think about her really quite a lot. And I suppose that's her soul, what she was like, the extraordinary sort of person she was.

So that's a form of eternal life?

Well . . . yes, eternal in the sense that it goes from one generation to another. The Jewish sense of eternal: from generation to generation. I'm happy with that.

(1993 conversation)

Jeanette Winterson

Widely regarded as one of the most exciting and innovative of writers of her generation, Jeanette Winterson has won many literary prizes for novels like *Oranges Are Not the Only Fruit* (1985), *The Passion* (1987), *Sexing the Cherry* (1989), *Gut Symmetries* (1997) and *The Powerbook* (2000).

In the beginning was the word, and it took the form of a book called Oranges Are Not the Only Fruit, *published when you were twenty-four. That was a classic work of life and art – but just encapsulate for us again the upbringing of the real Jeanette.*

I was adopted by Pentecostal evangelists in Accrington in the north, a grim factory town, one of those stolen from valleys and hills, and streets cut into it. My parents had a gospel tent and they used to go around the north west, usually to seaside resorts, put the tent up, get the harmonium out, and we'd preach and try and save souls. That was our life.

When you were a very little girl, did you imagine a picture of God?

Not as some sort of old guy from the Bible, no; but always as a solid, concrete presence – as somebody who was real. Because one of the good things about charismatic or evangelical religion is that it is not mediated: you don't feel distant from God. You feel that God is always close to you. Of course, that can get a bit cloying and suffocating, but I think the good side of it is that you feel that you are in a genuine relationship rather than in a relationship which is always removed.

Did you have any sense from other children you met that their life wasn't like that?

Certainly. I was always the odd one out at school because my real life was in the church, and I was desperate to get away from school so that I could carry on going to church. I went every night, and I used to walk because we were very poor. We had no car, we had no phone. So having walked the two miles each way to school every night, I would then walk the two miles each way to church, and thought nothing of it. Because to me, that was life. Of course, for a child, whatever you do is normal and natural to you. If you're brought up in that way, it seems perfectly reasonable and it's always everybody else that is peculiar.

What was that kind of faith? People who don't know – and I count myself among them – think of it as a very dour sort of religion, full of hell and damnation. Is that fair?

No, it's not. It was in many ways joyful and positive, in that this is a poor community and it's people who have come together, not in a literary way but in an oral way, testifying, talking about their life, talking about their difficulties – but finding a solution to those. Which, to me anyway, seems better than sitting in front of the television or going down to the pub. At least it was interactive, at least it was communal, and it was about the life of the spirit, which is so lost now in modern society. So when I look at it, I think maybe it's not such a bad thing. It's better that people should feel something deeply. It's better that they should have a life outside of what is simply material, than that we should worry about them being caught up in false religions or crazy sects.

So it's about passion?

Yes, which is so important. Life is so anodyne now, and we always try and shield ourselves from risk, which you can never do. We want guarantees for everything. Yet you can never shield yourself from the important things, the real things. I think religion is a way of saying to you, 'There are no guarantees except the one that you are loved by God, and from that everything else follows.'

You were preaching from the age of about twelve?

Because I was meant to be a missionary, you see. That was going to be my purpose in life, to go out and save the heathen. So naturally they wanted to start me early. Of course, in a way I've never given it up!

   I don't think it was brainwashing. I think it was a place where me and the outside world were constellated. It suits me. I am passionate by nature, and for me it was a good kind of upbringing, although it was difficult and traumatic and stressful and all of those things. It was also right for me, because it did teach me to appreciate invisible worlds, to appreciate the worlds of the soul and of the heart, and not simply to be caught up in that grim materialism. Of course, for poor people it's always been a way out, hasn't it, to say, 'No, this is not our life. Our life is other. Our life is somewhere else.'

I know that you didn't so much reject God, as a lot of people do when they're teenagers, as be rejected by the Church yourself. Tell me how that came about and how it felt.

I fell in love with another woman – well, she was a girl, because we were only fifteen – and because (guile isn't my stock-in-trade) I didn't hide it. It never occurred to me to hide it. I just thought that this was the most wonderful thing ever, told my parents. I was quite naive in a way. I suppose people would think, 'How could she be?' because we're so knowing. But I wasn't, and the way that I had been brought up made sure that I had a true kind of innocence. And I thought, 'I love you and that's all that matters.' So I told everybody, and of course then the boulders rained down! That really was fire and damnation. It was dreadful. I was threatened with all kinds of things and locked up and not allowed to go to school until I repented, subjected to exorcisms and tied up – all this kind of thing. Then it really got nasty and I had to choose. It was either leave home or leave her.

It must have been terribly lonely to be cast out from that family.

Yes, because it was an extended family. I mean, thank God I didn't have to spend too much time with Mrs Winterson because she was a tyrant, and my escape from her *was* the church and that large extended family where there were people who really did care about me. And I think a lot of people were sorry for what was happening, but they couldn't speak out.

Given the fact that you had this passionate belief in God and, as you said, a sort of innocent belief, did you ever think, 'Why did you let it happen?'

No. I was very angry, but I was still in a relationship with God. As long as you're angry, you're still talking, aren't you? So it wasn't that I thought, 'No, I've been betrayed and rejected and the heavens are as brass and there's nobody there.' I simply felt that these were things that I didn't understand and I would have to come to understand them. And I also began to learn then that God is religion-proof, and that God can persist in your life in spite of everything around you going completely wrong, and that being the fault of the Church.

So in a sense you moved away from organised religion, as it moved away from you, but you didn't move away from God.

No, I didn't. I used to shout at God all the time. And I tried to move away, but you can't move away from something which is all-pervasive. It's extremely difficult.

How quickly did art in general, and writing in particular, become a kind of substitute for religion?

I don't know that it did become a substitute. I think it had always worked in parallel with it, because the other thing that was banned in our house was books, because my mother thought that you never knew what was in books and they were subversive and inflammatory. There were only six books in the house and one of those was the Bible – not a lot of latitude there. And I used to get books from the library, but I was never allowed to keep any. Of course, one of the things I did do was to start to buy books secretly, and I had to hide them under my single bed. And anybody with a single bed, average size, and a paperback, average size, will discover that you can fit seventy-seven per layer under the mattress. But eventually, of course, my mother noticed that the mattress was rising visibly and that I was sleeping closer to the ceiling than to the floor. She discovered this and she took them all into the yard and she burned them. So it was not a separation. Art was there always, and art to me was liberatory. The books were doors. They were escape hatches I could go through. I discovered that literature was another world, and also that I was the kind of person who has need of another world.

And the kind of person who could create that other world – like Genesis!

Yes. One of the great things about living in an oral tradition is that you have to tell stories. Lots of people in our church couldn't read. My father can't read. So it was always about constructing narrative.

Your second novel – and you now describe it as a comedy, rather than a novel – was Boating for Beginners, *and it's a bizarre and hilarious take on the story of Noah. In this story, it's Noah who creates God out of ice cream. Was it that you had to debunk fundamentalism?*

Yes, I think so. Only I was asked if I could do a book for a comedy list that doesn't exist any more, with the publisher. I really wanted to, and I thought the Bible is a perfect subject, God's the perfect subject – coming at it, not in the way I did with *Oranges*, but really as a spoof, and making sense of my own dilemmas and contradictions, thinking, 'Do we create God or does God create us?' And I wanted to work with that.

In a way, the book has a serious undercurrent because it says there's a limit to what we can know, doesn't it?

I believe that. I'm always very sceptical of science, which wants the great answer to everything, because there is no great answer to everything. There's only a developing process of which we are a part, and we'll always be pushing at the rim of the universe.

It's true, and that's most certainly in that book in the most unexpected way, because it's through comedy. And I had the feeling that, like much of your work, it demonstrates that the kind of religion that you are proselytising, if indeed you might agree that you are, is one which is actually full of laughter.

Certainly. I think laughter is so important, and I think one of the relationships you can have with God is a jokey one, whereby if God contains everything, then God also contains laughter, and that should not be left out.

A lot of people say there's a sort of messianic streak in you and in your work. Can you say what you are messianic about?

You've got to *care*. You've got to be passionate in this life. If you're not here and you're not going to change anything, then what's the point? And that change is changing yourself, changing the world around you as best you can. There's that wonderful saying that everybody knows that it's better to light one candle than to rail against the darkness. I really believe that. And I want people to care. I want them to feel excited about life. I want them to feel that they *can* change things, that they're not simply passive consumers. And that's what's happening more and more. I suppose my message is, 'No. Find out who you are. Be active. Be passionate. Care about things. Make mistakes. Take risks. Be reckless. Get hurt. Break your heart. It doesn't matter. But take life by the scruff of the neck. Live it.'

And would you add to that, 'Look for God within yourself'?

Yes. I think God is to be found within the self, but I think there's also a dialogue with the outside world which is also a dialogue with God, in that you find manifestations of God everywhere. One of the lovely things about the Bible is that God is always appearing in the most unexpected places, and that happens both in the Old Testament and the New Testament. So the obvious places where God is to be found – in the synagogues or in the churches, even in the scrolls of the law – are not just where God is found. God is found among the ordinary people – at sea, on boats, in the market place, with the whores, with the sinners – so that God is fugitive from our authority. You know, we try and contain God and God always says, 'I'm not here, I'm somewhere else.'

There's a sentence in The Passion *in which the narrator says, 'I never go to confession. God doesn't want us to confess. He wants us to challenge him.' I wondered how you challenge God?*

I challenge God by asking what is my purpose on earth and how I can change that purpose, what I can be. I suppose it's keeping up that dialogue and not letting God off the hook, not being satisfied with saying, 'OK, well, if you're the creator, now we've just got to get on with it.' It's about saying, 'Well, you've created this, so you too are involved, God. You can't just let it go. You still have to be there,' and trying to work with that dynamic. I suppose it's a sense of God as highest value, rather than God as some person or authority.

I was going to ask you if you thought of God as male or female, because for some people that's a very important question.

Yes, it is. I suppose I don't think of God as either male or female, I really don't. Obviously I was brought up with the idea of a male god, but that never seemed to make much sense. And so now, when I think about God, I do think about God as a totality.

Do you blame God for things that go wrong? I don't mean things that go wrong in your own life, because that might seem to be petty, but for disasters. It's that old problem of pain, the problem of evil. How do you address that?

I don't think that evil is the absence of good. I think that evil is a palpable force and I think it's real and I think it's in its own right. It's very distressing, isn't it, because certainly in the Old Testament you get some very odd texts – particularly the book of Job – about what God is capable of, and it would appear that God (himself or herself) is capable of fantastic evil, and the idea of a split between God and the Devil is just a way of describing two parts of the same process. I'm sure that's true.

There's a very strange bit in Job, isn't there, where God actually has to hide himself under the throne – kind of *from* himself – because he's in such a rage. You just think, 'What is going on here? God is hiding from God' – which seems to me to be a very complex relationship in a very complex set of ideas; and that's why I say that we are involved in a challenge – us, God, the universe – the whole thing is something which is still developing, still in tension. It's dynamic. It's not passive. It's not a created universe and then an absentee god. It is something which is still happening to us. It is this engagement that I love.

Do you still read the Bible?

Endlessly. It's by my bedside.

Do you read it for stories or for guidance?

Both. It's good at both. I love the way that it condenses narrative so that in just a few verses you get the story, you get a moral, you know who the characters are. I've used it to keep my style very tight because I don't like this verbal incontinence which is the fashion nowadays. The Bible's very good at avoiding that, so it was an excellent 'manual', I suppose. But I also read it because it's so fascinating, and it is comforting. When you read, 'Let not your hearts be troubled, neither let them be afraid,' you feel comforted – not in a way which is redundant, but you think, 'Yes, my heart *is* troubled. Why am I afraid?' And you can begin to ask yourself those questions and find solace there, and peace there – which I do.

And do you pray?

Sometimes there's nothing you can do but pray. And I think prayer does shift things. Whether it simply unblocks the self in some sort of therapeutic way, or whether you do channel into energies which are outside of yourself and very powerful, I don't know. But I know that prayer makes a difference. For me, being a control freak, there are times when I say, 'There's nothing I can do, but what I can do is pray.'

I was thinking of the 1990s . . . you went through a period which was quite tough. You were done over by quite a few critics and there was a kind of backlash against your success. Some might say you brought some of it on yourself, but whatever – I don't want to go back over that history – those experiences are very painful. Those of us who've gone through them know that. And at that sort of time in your life, do you actively seek comfort from your faith?

Yes. And one of the things that I did do – I sold up in London and I fled to the country, and it was rather like going to some unhaunted desert place. I thought, 'I will try and get back to the core of what matters underneath all this sound and fury, believing in what I'm for.' Because, of course, my parents had my missionary purpose, but I believe that I'm for something, and I believe that what I'm meant to do is to write, is to try and get underneath people's assumptions, is to try and find a natural language for the sublime, is to try and push forward imagination. I think that's what I'm here for. And at that point I was losing all sense of it, and I thought, 'Well, God will settle me in this, or I will discover that it was never genuine at all.' And so I waited. I waited for the still small voice, without hope, without fear, in a very passive state – which, again, is not like me, because I just love to get out there and do things. I did find that core again. I went right back down into that stillness, and I do believe that there is a God-centred stillness.

And what happened then?

I started work again. I couldn't work for about two years. It was dreadful. And then I began to find that sort of creative joyfulness, and I'd come through a very black space. And I thought, 'This is good because now I will go on. Something important has happened.' You know, you arrive at the boundaries of common sense, and either you turn back or you cross over. I think we have to go all through these things, these dark nights of the soul which religion talks so well about, and there is nobody to help you. Again, the book of Job: you feel that you are deserted and abandoned by everyone, and yet you hold on to that core, and you simply go on believing, even though there's nothing to believe in.

And you did actually reach that blackest point?

Oh yes. It was complete breakdown. Not being able to work for me is like not being able to see. I saw just nothing but blackness.

You lost your faith in yourself. You lost your faith in your art. But did you actually lose your faith in God, ever?

I no longer knew what God was. I no longer knew. It was so catatonic. It was like being in a padded cell without any sensory experience, and just believing that you did exist but having no way of really confirming that, I suppose. It's typical nervous breakdown stuff, and that deep depression. It did pass, and all I could do at the time was pray in a very feeble fashion, which I suppose condensed would be, 'Save me!'

Was human life any consolation?

None, absolutely none. My friends were great and my partner was wonderful. But I was hell to live with and I don't think another human being can shoulder that. It's too big a burden. In the end, the real problems are always with yourself and you are always alone with that self. Although other people can guide you and coax you and advise you, if you can't move through it then it becomes very artificial, anybody else's help. It's just temporary. It has to come from somewhere very deep, I think.

You use the word 'self', and it seems to me from reading you that you believe that the idea of God, and the spirit, is very much within everybody, whether they know it or not. A lot of people don't know, as you've said. How should people – and a lot of us are seeking – set about finding that spiritual side?

It's different for all sorts of people. Some people can do it through art, because art is so evocative of deep feeling. I think one of our problems is that our feelings can be very superficial because of the way that we live, and what we're trying to get at is some authenticity, something which is real. So perhaps to be moved by pictures or books or music is a way of refocusing your own energy so that you are more receptive and you're able to hear God, or to see God. I think the problem often is, it's not the transmitter, it's us as receivers which are faulty.

Do you think that the secular life that most of us lead, and the particular barrage of the media-saturated world we live in, cuts us off even more from the spiritual side?

Certainly. I think it muffles us to real things, and I think it neuters any genuine sense of whatever is outside the material. That's very bad. You can go to somewhere – a poor Catholic place like Anacapri, a little village that's on Capri where I go every year because I love

Capri – and they are so committed to their faith in a way which is unquestioning, but also rather beautiful. When I go into the church to pray, there is a real sense of God because, of course, they are part of God. So you feel that it is a living faith.

There's a passage in Sexing the Cherry *which I found very interesting. The narrator says, 'The Buddhists say there are 149 ways to God. I am not looking for God, only for myself, and that is far more complicated. God has a great deal written about him. Nothing has been written about me. God is bigger, like my mother, easier to find, even in the dark. I could be anywhere, and since I can't describe myself, I can't ask for help. We are alone in this quest. I've met a great many pilgrims on their way towards God, and I wonder why they have chosen to look for him rather than themselves. Perhaps I'm missing the point. Perhaps while looking for someone else, you might come across yourself un-expectedly, but they don't seem to care who they are. Some of them have said to me that the very point of searching for God is to forget about oneself, to lose oneself forever.'*
    Am I right in saying that that sort of ascetic abnegation of self has no appeal to you?

None whatsoever. Indeed, I think one of the triumphs of the Christian message is its individuality. It is about you, the person, taking responsibility both for your own life and for your search for God, that you have a soul and God cares about it, and it's worth saving. That's rather wonderful, but it is an individual journey. It's not one that can be made *en masse.* At present we're not very keen on taking individual responsibility. We want governments to decide for us. We always want somebody else to do the thinking, whereas any search for God involves a deep knowledge of self. You can't avoid yourself if you're looking for God.

I suppose there are people who would say that that is very self-absorbed and that the Buddhist way, the Zen way of actually forgetting self, is actually a higher purpose. What would you say to that?

I think it's a paradox. When you do anything that's meaningful, you do forget yourself because you become contained within the work. I think, for instance, that all art is actually a collaboration. Though the artist is a supreme creator, that kind of renaissance through to a romantic ideal, it's rather that you are collaborating with your subject, whether you're painting it or writing about it. In a way, most people try and hold back from that genuine collaboration. They want to stay at a copying distance. And you can't in life. You have to risk it. So for me it is about consciously saying, 'Yes, I'll take the risk. I'll jump in. I'll forget everything. I'll do this.' But then within that consciousness comes that lack of consciousness which allows you to become part of what you are doing.

Your writing takes risks. So, in a sense, you're demonstrating that every time you write, aren't you?

Yes. Just because you've written one book doesn't mean that you can write another. There are no guarantees, and you always have to push yourself further and try not to be repetitive. Because I think it's only that emotional questing that allows you to be genuine in your work and not simply to be a kind of reproduction. I hate reproductions, whether it's furniture or pictures, and I don't want to reproduce myself.

Can you imagine ever going through that very bad time again? No matter what happened, you might write a book where people choose to be extremely nasty about you. Can you imagine it affecting you so badly again, or do you think you've found the strength to overcome that?

It won't happen like that again. You do fight these battles and you do win them. That one's over with. But there will be other things. We want instant fixes and we can't have them. The whole of life is this endless quest where things will be painful, difficult, dangerous, risky. Sometimes they'll be ecstatically happy. Sometimes it will be full of meaning. Sometimes it will be dead. But that's what life is. That's its richness, its pattern. And I know I'm going to have a terrible time in the future – of course I will, because only that will bring me new insights, will help me to grow. I don't fear it. And having come through it once in that way, I know that it is beneficial. I know that it is worthwhile and I know that it makes you stronger . . .

. . . I don't go to church. I think the Church of England is finished in this country, and I obviously can't go back to any of the evangelical sects, partly because they don't really respect or appreciate the intellect, and I need that. I need the totality of faith. I can't do all this 'don't think about it, just accept it'. Of course you have to think about it. Think about things day and night. I can't be a Catholic for obvious reasons, though that is rather seductive, and I think if I do end up in Italy, I probably will just go to the Catholic church all the time. It wasn't in my background at all. Far from it. The whole Protestant ethic of smashing up statues and doing away with anything which seems to be symbolic, I think is rather impoverished, because I think we do need the symbolic life, and to me religion is about the symbolic life. So I like all that. I like the incense, I like the ritual, I like the way that you have to communicate with the priest, with each other, through the language.

I happen to know that you love opera and ballet. In a sense, you could see it as an extension of the aesthetic.

Yes. There's that marvellous scene at the end of Act One of *Tosca*, isn't there, where they all fill up the church and the music's really going at it and they've got this bell ringing in the background, and the cannons go off. Scarpia kneels down and says, 'Tosca, you make me forget God!' The curtain comes down and you think, 'Wow!'

Moments like that in great art – do you feel a sort of transcendence? Does that take you out of yourself?

Yes, it does. I feel it is the kick of joy in the universe, and it's accessible and it's about living beyond the confines of your own life and suddenly connecting with something much bigger than you – this real power and energy which is, of course, what you channel down for your work. But sometimes it just explodes out of you, too. I love that. And I do thank God every day when I get up. To whom – I don't know – I just say, 'Thank you for my life.' Simple as that. I just do that every morning.

(2002 conversation)